FOSTER CHILD

FOSTER CHILD

A Biography of Jodie Foster

BUDDY FOSTER

and Leon Wagener

A DUTTON BOOK

DUTTON
Published by the Penguin Group
Penguin Books USA Inc., 375 Hudson Street, New York, New York 10014, U.S.A.
Penguin Books Ltd, 27 Wrights Lane, London W8 5TZ, England
Penguin Books Australia Ltd, Ringwood, Victoria, Australia
Penguin Books Canada Ltd, 10 Alcorn Avenue, Toronto, Ontario, Canada M4V 3B2
Penguin Books (N.Z.) Ltd, 182–190 Wairau Road, Auckland 10, New Zealand

Penguin Books Ltd, Registered Offices: Harmondsworth, Middlesex, England

First published by Dutton, an imprint of Dutton Signet,
a division of Penguin Books USA Inc.
Distributed in Canada by McClelland & Stewart Inc.

First Printing, May, 1997
10 9 8 7 6 5 4 3 2 1

 REGISTERED TRADEMARK—MARCA REGISTRADA

LIBRARY OF CONGRESS CATALOGING-IN-PUBLICATION DATA:

Foster, Buddy
    Foster child / Buddy Foster and Leon Wagener
      p.   cm.
    "A Dutton book"
    ISBN 0-525-94143-6 (acid free paper)
    1. Foster, Jodie. 2. Motion picture actors and actresses—United States—Biography.
    3. Motion picture producers and directors—United States—Biography. 4. Foster, Buddy. 1957–
    I. Wagener, Leon. II. Title.
    PN2287.F624F67 1997
    791.43'028'092—dc21
        [B]   97-3947
                                                                        CIP

Printed in the United States of America
Set in Transitional 521
Designed by Eve L. Kirch

In Memory of
Josephine Dominguez-Hill

INTRODUCTION

It has been said fame is a curse. At first hand I have seen the truth of this. Over the past thirty years my sister Jodie Foster has been victimized by stalkers, pilloried by the press, sometimes cruelly harassed by paparazzi, and mercilessly discussed by gossipmongers who have never met her and know nothing about her.

As a teenager I starred in a hit network TV series, appeared on the covers of magazines, and was nearly torn apart by frenzied fans while appearing in a holiday parade. In the end I fled Hollywood.

Jodie persisted and prevailed. No matter how mean-spirited the director, cold the temperature at five A.M. cast calls, heartless the reviews, or chaotic our home life, Jodie has soldiered on. Watching her over the years—through the crazed roller-coaster ride that was her childhood, during her early career, her brushes with death at the hands of obsessed fans, and the triumph of her two Academy Award Best Actress awards—I have been overwhelmingly proud and sometimes astonished. I have drawn strength from her example when I felt weak and constant inspiration from her firm resolve.

The saga of the Foster family is sometimes horrifying but in the end exultant. It is a quintessentially American and specifically Southern Californian story. It probably couldn't have happened in any other place or at any other time.

We were unlikely candidates for show business careers. Our mother was a Midwesterner who grew up during World War II dreaming of becoming a jazz singer. She knew no one in Hollywood and hadn't a single relative who had been a performer. But she had a dream and somehow knew the place for dreamers in those days was California. Like millions of others, she sensed that there was magic at the end of our great continent. She arrived when the Golden State was undergoing an unprecedented explosion of growth. For better or worse, orange groves were being plowed under at the rate of thousands of acres a day. The burgeoning new television industry was a hungry beast in desperate need of new talent. It was a time when hard work and a refusal to give up turned ordinary people into millionaires, rocket scientists, and movie stars.

Other books have been written about Jodie Foster, and more will undoubtedly be written in the future. But none of the other writers grew up with her and shared her life. None of them understand the will and perseverance it took for her to overcome daunting obstacles in her personal and professional life to make it to stardom.

I have grown uncomfortable over the years with the distortions and out-and-out lies that have been written about my sister and feel it is time to set the record straight. Jodie and my family have been extremely reticent about letting the public look into our private lives in any way. I understand that and generally agree with them. But over the years I have discovered that the press and public inevitably fill such a breach however they wish. I've learned not to read any of the so-called interviews with Jodie. They usually torture and twist her words pretzel-like to make it appear that she is saying whatever they wanted her to say in the first place. Even television interviews are severely edited and tend to be heavy with voice-over. After years of frustration I was given the opportunity to write this book, and I decided the time was right. Enough years have passed since our childhood and early struggles to put some perspective on the pain and to see the heroic dimension on everyone's part. It was a hard struggle to survive. But we did and should be proud of that.

I know that my parents and three sisters will sometimes disagree with my recollections. We all see life through the prism of our own experiences and expectations. But I hope all will agree I have been fair and have been harder on myself than on anyone else.

ONE

I go for complexity, and usually the truth is complex. —JODIE FOSTER

When my sister Jodie Foster strode up to the stage of the Dorothy Chandler Pavilion to accept her Best Actress Oscar for *Silence of the Lambs* in 1992, millions of people around the world witnessed a transformation. The sweet little girl they had first known in a Coppertone ad, the daring teenager who had starred in *Alice Doesn't Live Here Anymore* and *Taxi Driver*, the Yale honors student, and the frightened stalking victim of John Hinckley, Jr., had emerged as an actor of the first rank.

By winning her second Academy Award in four years, Jodie became a major player in Hollywood. She quickly launched Egg, her own production company, and turned her hand to writing, directing, producing, or starring in such acclaimed and successful movies as *Nell* and *Home for the Holidays*. She was given millions of dollars to spend with an independence that rivals that of Barbra Streisand or Robert Redford, figures many years her senior. It was an extraordinary position for a woman who was only thirty years old at the time, evidence of Hollywood's hard-won confidence that Jodie is one of the elite in the entertainment business.

At the moment the Oscar was announced, I was watching our mother, Brandy. Her eyes were red, her face a mask of tension until she dissolved into tears of joy and relief. For so many years Mom had been part of Jodie's career, shepherding her to auditions and shoots, battling alongside Jodie for the parts my sister wanted, and sometimes against Jodie's own, very determined ideas about where her career should lead. I knew my mother well enough to realize that this second Oscar was the proof to her as well that Jodie was a legend, not a fluke child star unable to make the transition to an adult career.

Since nearly thirty years before, when my own career as a model and then actor began, our family had viewed show business as a contest. At first the prize was relief from financial desperation. For me it always remained simply a way to make a living, one that I left when the benefits were overwhelmed by the costs. But for Jodie acting became a consuming obsession, not because of the money it brought but because she learned at an early age that she could master anything she tried. She has always craved challenges, and nothing else she has ever encountered can match the challenge of a sterling performance.

In the midst of all the celebration and excitement of that Oscar for *Silence*, Jodie reminded me of how demanding her standards are. Our family had watched the ceremony at Rex II Ristorante, a posh eatery in downtown Los Angeles where Orion Pictures was hosting its party for all the major people involved in the movie. Jodie arrived to confront a sea of paparazzi that had to be parted by a wedge of bodyguards. Inside Rex, the cast and crew of *Silence* were celebrating with loud shouts and glasses of champagne. Everyone was caught up in the triumph. Not only had Jodie won Best Actress, but also *Silence* had garnered the Best Actor award for her costar, Anthony Hopkins, Best Director for Jonathan Demme, and Best Picture. That hadn't happened since 1975, when *One Flew Over the Cuckoo's Nest* brought in all four.

As Jodie came toward me, I saw the glow of victory in her eyes that reminded me so clearly of how far she had come. We hugged tearfully and made a moment's small talk, until she told me what had been going through her mind as she sat waiting for the announcement of the winner.

"Remember at the end of the movie, when I'm being stalked by the killer in the dark and he's wearing infrared glasses?" she shouted above the roar of the crowd. "Well, you can see a shadow as he passes by me. Don't you get it? It's supposed to be pitch dark in that room, but you can clearly see a shadow!"

It stunned me that at such a moment she would think of a tiny technical flaw, one she had no responsibility for, one that hardly anyone but she would have noticed. Yet from the beginning of her career, Jodie has been a perfectionist. She expects perfection of herself, and she expects it to be mirrored in everything associated with her. It's a part of her character that was reinforced every day in the household where we grew up.

I could only smile and say, "Well, it's only up from here."

She mouthed the words, "I know," and I remembered that the flip side of her perfectionism has always been her incredible confidence in herself.

Jodie then sounded another familiar theme. She was thinking about breaking her business relationship with Mom, gracefully suggesting a deserved retirement. This, she said, was part of a serious lifestyle change that might mean quitting acting for a while and maybe even returning to the academic life she had so enjoyed: "I'm seriously considering enrolling in the master's–Ph.D. program at Yale and getting a doctorate in European literature.

"You know as well as I do," she went on, "acting started out as a hobby and then became a fun thing that made me money. It was never meant to be my life's work; this movie-star thing isn't really me. I'm not a movie star anyway. I'm an actor. Maybe I'll just direct and produce and stay behind the scenes most of the time."

In both public interviews and private conversations, Jodie gives mixed signals about acting. She speaks of it as a hobby, something to do, something she fell into. She does not relish the baggage of fame. Yet her professional demeanor on the set and the intensity with which she drives herself and others show that she is completely committed to her work. If Jodie often tells friends, family, and the public that she is thinking about getting out of the business, earning a graduate degree, hiking through the Rockies, or living in Paris while she translates Baudelaire, it's because she wants people to know that acting is a choice for her, not something she does simply to accumulate millions of dollars. She wants us all to see significance in what she chooses to do. Jodie has a vision of what her work should reveal. That vision was in large part shaped by our upbringing, both its good and bad aspects.

Jodie and I understand each other in ways few siblings can. For one thing, we were both successful child actors, part of an exclusive club with doses of gut-wrenching rejection mixed with the intoxicating rush of fame. With a strong, stable home life, a kid can be successfully sheltered from the crazy highs and lows of show business. But our family life could charitably be termed chaotic. In a recent interview with the *New York Times*, Jodie darkly alluded to our problems, saying: "I came from tragedies," but refused to elaborate to a startled reporter.

It's a story that some members of my family would prefer were never told, but my strong conviction is that it will be therapeutic for us all. Jodie and what drives her cannot be understood without knowing about her early life. Growing up on the set of TV series such as *Mayberry R.F.D.*, in which I costarred and Jodie made her series TV debut, we were aware, even as children, of the irony of working by day in an *Ozzie and Harriet* world but coming home at night to our own version of *The Addams Family*.

Jodie was the last of Lucius Fisher Foster III and Evelyn "Brandy" Foster's four children. Their eldest daughter, Lucinda (a variation of my father's name), though she was always called Cindy, was born in 1954. Connie (named after Dad's mother, Constance) came along in 1955, followed by me in 1957. I was named Lucius Fisher Foster IV, though I have always been known as Buddy. Jodie, born Alicia Christian, came last, on November 19, 1962, more than three years after our parents' divorce papers were first filed in Los

Angeles Superior Court. That spared her much of the parental warfare her older siblings were forced to endure. By the time she arrived, our parents' marriage was over, and most of their horrific battles had already been waged.

The news that Jodie was on the way was exciting to Connie, Cindy, and me. I can still remember the day, when my mother was about five months pregnant, that we each had a chance to put our heads to her stomach and listen to the baby in her womb. I was certain that this baby—of course it would be a little brother—was going to be my best friend. Focusing on Mom's pregnancy was, for all of us, a way of forgetting the tumult of our lives.

But later that week came one of the worst blowups between our parents. It started with a terrifying banging at the front door. We all knew from bitter experience that the angry, insistent hammering meant trouble. Dad was back, and he was obviously furious. He demanded that Mom let him in, which she defiantly refused to do. So he smashed the door nearly off the hinges, snapping the lock assembly, and roared in. Instantly, Mom changed from nurturer to fierce defender of the pack. She counterattacked with a barrage of obscenities and a hail of dishes, ashtrays, and whatever other missiles she could launch.

"Get out of here, Lucius, you son of a bitch! You don't belong here," she roared.

I dove into my usual storm shelter, a round table covered with a white cloth, from which I could observe without being seen. Mom appeared to be completely out of her mind. Fearless despite being pregnant, she fought with a vengeance. Dad put up his hands to protect himself from her blows.

Then I got the biggest shock of my life. Out of my mother's bedroom emerged a woman with only a white towel wrapped around her. She had close-cropped hair and dark skin. I had no idea she was even in the house. In her right hand was a gun, purposefully aimed in my father's direction. The woman strode over to my father and deliberately, coolly, held the gun right against his forehead.

"You get the fuck out of here or I'll blow your brains out," she hissed in a gruff Spanish accent.

I later learned the gun was a .25-caliber semiautomatic, but to me it looked like John Wayne's Colt .45. When the Los Angeles police finally arrived, they removed the bullets from the gun's clip and returned it to the woman. Dad promised he would pay to fix the front door and left, likely with a great sigh of relief.

Only then did I realize I had wet my pants. From under the table, I looked at my mother's gun-wielding friend with both awe and fear, wondering if she was a savior or another menace. Fortunately, she was the former. Josephine Dominguez Hill, or Aunt Jo, as we all came to know her, moved into our home that same day, bringing her son, Chris, two years younger than me. He became my best friend and, later, Jodie's sole playmate. Though it was years before any of us kids grasped the complete significance of the relationship, Aunt Jo was my mother's lover and had been for several years.

Aunt Jo was full of passionate love for us kids. Her support, both moral and economic, gave us a chance to survive. She was truly our second parent. In my father's absence Aunt Jo was very much like a father to us. She took me to my first baseball game and gave us all advice on everything from sex to schoolwork. We were so attached to Aunt Jo, who was called Jo D., for Jo Dominguez, that my baby sister was called Jodie in her honor.

Through the years that Aunt Jo supported seven people on her meager income from work as an inspector in the aviation industry, we were always aware of how little money we had. It was in stark contrast to our earlier years. Although we had to endure unending battles between Mom and Dad, we had at least lived well. The first house I remember was the one at the top of Fairfax Drive, near Laurel Canyon, a comfortable 1930s Spanish mission-style place. We had brilliant views of Los Angeles and the city's shimmering carpet of lights at night. The hardwood floors were covered with Persian rugs. It had round arches in the hallways and was decorated in Mom's usual good taste with Herman Miller furniture and leather couches. The street was a cul-de-sac that my sisters and I, as well as a neighborhood filled with children, used as a playground.

The house was beautiful, but life was not. Dad was rarely home, and when he was around there was constant strife. He always seemed to have a simmering rage whenever he was with Mom, who possessed a penchant for setting it off. Inevitably when they were together, ugly fights would occur; he yelled at us, then railed at Mom. She thundered back, often throwing things. Then Dad would leave. Often my sisters and I were made to feel guilty for his abrupt departures. On the unusual occasions Dad was home long enough to have a meal with us, we would wish he was not. Once, when I was just a tot, I spilled a glass of milk at the table. He leaped to his feet, yelling: "Brandy, can't you control these goddamn kids? This is why I can't stay in this house!"

Mom would bait him in front of us, often bringing up his

philandering during dinner. He would plead with her to talk about it behind closed doors, not in the presence of the children. But she insistently, gleefully, pushed his hot buttons.

Our parents' marriage, which began with a New Year's celebration in Tijuana, Mexico, in 1954, lasted only five tumultuous years, though it limped along for several more before the divorce decree was final. As with most warring couples, they had different versions as to why the marriage unraveled. To this day my mother claims it was Dad's philandering, while he blames her lesbian affair.

Dad still denies his womanizing tore the marriage apart, and he's right in the sense that it was only one factor. But my earliest memories are filled with the furor and pain it caused. Even up until the time she was pregnant with Jodie and the marriage was long finished, Mom occasionally cruised the streets of Los Angeles hunting for Dad, smoking cigarettes and seething with anger and frustration. Sometimes, in the chill of early morning, Mom would pull Cindy, Connie, and me out of bed, put us in the back of our white Ford Fairlane, and drive to his office or girlfriends' houses.

In the early days she was hoping to catch him red-handed. We prayed she would not. But later she accosted him to insist he pay child support. Inevitably she found him, and frequently he was with another woman. One horrible night we caught him in front of his real estate office on Sunset Boulevard, arm in arm with a woman. When Mom and the woman saw each other, it was as though some primordial instinct took over. They circled and pounced. Mom screamed like a maniac, swinging, kicking, scratching, and punching her nemesis of the moment, who later became Dad's third wife. He just looked on, apparently amused.

Throughout the ordeal my sisters and I sobbed helplessly in the backseat of the car. That was one of the rare times when we three siblings weren't fighting among ourselves. We were too scared.

These continual fights even included a kidnapping. Years after the day Aunt Jo had entered our lives like some television sheriff, my mother told me that her lover had pulled the gun on Dad because she feared he might take me or my sisters away. Several months previously, he had done just that during a time of bitter quarreling over alimony and the division of their property. His lawyer apparently came up with a scheme they hoped would force Mom to give in to all of Dad's demands. One weekend our father had custody of us, and he and his lawyer refused to give us back.

Connie and Cindy were enrolled in a Catholic convent. I was taken to the lawyer's house for safe keeping, because I was only four and too young to be put in a school. Quite naturally, I became hysterical and couldn't stop crying. Dad's lawyer got very angry with me, making my panic that much worse. Unsure what to do, he pushed me in a dark closet, locked the door, and kept me there for what seemed like hours. Ever after when playing hide-and-seek, I was unable to hide in closets without experiencing a sense of drowning, of being unable to escape some terrible impending fate.

Over the next few days, our mother, frantic but determined, found the convent school, stormed in, and retrieved her daughters. One of the nuns who attempted to stop her discovered that although Mom was not quite five feet tall, she had the strength of a linebacker. Brandy grabbed the nun by the habit, lifted her completely off the ground, and snarled: "Get in my way and I'll beat the crap out of you!" Soon afterward, she was also able to recover me.

The kidnapping incident is a prime example of my parents' selective and utterly contradictory perspectives on our family history. Mom vehemently insists Dad took us away as a blackmail ploy. She says he wanted her to agree to a smaller alimony settlement, and that was his way of forcing the issue. We were always told he paid no child support and aided us not at all, that we were on the verge of starvation all the time. Yet he swears to this day that he has stacks of cancelled checks with Mom's signature on them.

Dad's version is that he knew she was having a lesbian affair and flaunting it in front of us. He says that at the time he thought Brandy was an unfit mother, and he was convinced he was doing the right thing to get us away from her.

My mother's version of how she got pregnant with Jodie also challenges Dad's characterization of the support he gave us or his concern for our welfare. It is harrowing and, frankly, rings true to me. My mother filed for divorce on August 3, 1959. In court papers she said the separation had taken place on July 28, and that the marriage had lasted five years, seven months, and twenty-five days. Dad refused to respond to it, so the divorce was finalized within two years, and Mom was awarded a hundred dollars per child in monthly support.

It was a mantra of our childhoods that Dad gave the money grudgingly and far from every month. The most obvious evidence was the fact that after the divorce, our standard of living plummeted. We soon moved from the showy house in the hills down to a working-class neighborhood in "the flats," occupying the cramped upper floor of a duplex on

Hamel Street, where Dad would break down the door that terrifying day. The house was in the shadow of Cedars of Lebanon Hospital; ambulances wailed by at all hours. Even staying there required constant juggling of finances. Mom was forced to go to desperate lengths just to keep us fed and a roof over our heads. More than once she pawned her diamond ring. Time and again she begged Dad to help us.

Mom told *Parade* magazine in 1976: "I found myself running to his real estate office, pleading for the support money. 'I have to have this and have to have that.' As any divorced wife knows, it's a very humiliating position, like a dog begging for a bone. I would have to create a big scene, stage a tantrum. Then I would be given enough to tide me over for that period."

On one of these trips, she went to his office on Sunset Boulevard, demanding he pay up. She told me he brought her into his office and said: "If you take off your clothes and let me fuck you, I'll give you all of it." She said the act frankly meant nothing to her, and she needed the money to buy food for her three children. So she did it with him right on the desk. Then she grabbed his wallet, took all the money he had, and left.

"Fuck yourself now, you bastard," she yelled and slammed the door.

But proving good can come from bad, Mom discovered she was pregnant with Jodie soon afterward, and in our misery we had something to look forward to. When the time came, Aunt Jo went to the hospital with Mom. But she didn't sit in the waiting room and nervously pace back and forth, as was expected of husbands in the early sixties. Instead, she stayed right in the delivery room with Mom—

coaching, reassuring, and offering moral support through what became a life-and-death struggle for mother and child.

Mom, who had just turned thirty-four, went through a hellish thirty-six hour labor because Jodie was turned in the wrong direction. As the ordeal continued, hour after excruciating hour, both of their heart rates began decelerating alarmingly, and the doctor decided that a cesarean section was necessary. After making an incision in Mom's intestinal wall, he discovered the situation was even more desperate than he had thought. The umbilical cord was wrapped around Jodie's neck, cutting her oxygen supply and turning her blue. The interminable medical drama finally ended in triumph, but not before the tiny flame that was Jodie's life perilously flickered. After the birth, Mom was told she should never try to have another child.

A week after the birth, when Jodie and Mom were finally strong enough to come home, Aunt Jo drove them from the hospital. As they came up the walk, Jo carrying Jodie in one arm and lending the other to Mom, Brandy looked weary but jubilant. And Jo was as proud as any parent could have been.

TWO

How can you rebel against your parents when you are your parents?
—JODIE FOSTER

he landscape of my sisters' and my childhood was shaped
by three adults, two of them often locked in pitched
conflict, the third a haven of stability. Each came from
completely different worlds. As I've grown older, and in the
course of researching this book, I've come to understand a
great deal about the forces that made our mother and father
and Aunt Jo the people they were.

My mother is a fighter, a woman who protects and
defends the things she loves instinctively, sometimes
without thought for the consequences. She resents heavy-
handed authority—though she was a tyrant herself—and
she doesn't take much on trust. She's had plenty of lessons
that have taught her not to. My father is also a fighter.
Though he has a strong sense of honor, he took a long time
to take his responsibility to his family seriously. The children

from his early marriages were expected to fend for themselves because that is what he had been forced to do.

As a pair they provided their children with a rocky start in many ways, though perhaps it was no worse than what either of them had endured on their own. Thankfully, we had Aunt Jo as well. The drama of her initial appearance in our lives proved to be the exception, not the rule. She brought a calm and steady strength to our lives, something we truly needed. Sadly, she died in 1984, but her influence on all of us was tremendous. Her story belongs here, too.

Our biological maternal grandmother was a tragic figure named Josie Almond. She was born in Rockford, Illinois, but her family later moved to Brooklyn, New York. In her youth she was a plump, full-breasted Irish girl with dark curly hair, light blue eyes, and a dazzling smile—all of which our mother inherited.

In 1928, although the Great Depression was less than a year away, business was still booming, and the streets of Brooklyn were teeming with immigrants from all over Europe.

In these giddy times Josie had a secret life and a secret lover. Her paramour was a much older, successful Wall Street broker of German extraction. Grandmother Josie was shattered the day she learned what she had most feared; she was going to have a child out of wedlock. When she told her parents, they were appalled. A council of family elders was convened to decide her fate and that of her child. After much arguing, a decision was made. The family would pretend nothing was out of order until Josie began to show. Then she would be sequestered in the house with the excuse of illness, so the neighbors would not gossip. Then the baby would be sent away.

Unfortunately, I can only speculate as to why the obvious solution of marriage was ruled out. Perhaps the father was already married and paid off Grandma's family to keep silent and send the child halfway cross the country to be raised. Or maybe the social stigma against cross-ethnic marriages was too strict to overcome, and he was never even told he had fathered a child.

My mother was born Evelyn Della Almond on September 21, 1928, in the Bronx. Soon after her birth she was taken from her mother forever and brought to Rockford, Illinois, where she was raised by Lucy Lefler Almond and her husband, John L. Almond, Jr., a postman, who was a cousin. Lucy had been born in Rockford on March 19, 1896, to George and Elnora Lefler. Childless at thirty-two, she took to adoptive motherhood with a sense of purpose. Devoutly religious, Lucy proved to be a loving but no-nonsense parent. Her child-rearing philosophy of "spare the rod and spoil the child" was one my mother learned well.

From the time she was old enough to walk, Evelyn was made to obey rigid rules of etiquette and behavior. Even an accidental miscue was punished. Mom has generally avoided telling tales of her tumultuous upbringing, except to say resentfully how miserable it was. One anecdote she relates with relish, however, concerns how she got the nickname Brandy. I suppose she likes the story because it represents one of the first times she defied her stern parents.

As a very young child, Mom got into the supply of brandy, kept for medicinal purposes. After a few snorts she wandered into the living room, where she danced a jig, and then fell fast asleep. Apparently, her little performance was so amusing no punishment was meted out. The Almonds simply moved the jug to a higher shelf and renamed Mom after the liquor; the incident was never mentioned again.

In the early forties, Rockford swelled to double its size as the U.S. Army reception center Camp Grant filled with recruits bound for war. In her early teens, Mom was physically precocious and had a keen eye for men. Perhaps preoccupied by her frisky charge, Lucy failed to notice what Mom and apparently the neighbors were all too aware of: that her husband was having an affair with a pretty neighbor named Helen.

Mom later told Dad with bitterness that she had often watched from her bedroom window as the two signaled each other with hand waving, indicating the coast was clear for a midnight liaison. When John Almond finally ran off with his paramour, Lucy was the only one surprised. To Mom it was an early lesson in the treachery of men. When I learned about John Almond's abandoning his family for another woman, I understood much better her fury toward our father's running around.

Other branches of the Almond family took in Lucy and Mom until Lucy was able to get a job working for the Barber Coleman Company, which manufactured machine tools, where she became a foreman. At the factory she met Charles Schmidt, a machinist who worked under her. He became her second husband, proving far more loyal than John Almond, staying with Lucy until his death in 1962.

An indifferent student, Mom graduated from Roosevelt Junior High in 1942. During the summer of that year she scandalized Rockford by publicly smooching a black man in the backseat of a car, plus being a sexy little hell-raiser in general. She was a knockout, too much for her stepfather.

Mom has always professed a love of handsome men in uniforms. I remember riding in the backseat of our Ford Fairlane and watching the look on Mom's face when she saw a man in uniform. That gorgeous smile of hers would light up, and she would beam from ear to ear. She always said she thought that men in uniform were the most distinguished and honorable of men.

However, when gossip about Mom's fascination with uni-formed men—and particularly a black one—became the talk of the machine shop, Charlie Schmidt decided something had to be done. On September 8, 1942, as *Casablanca* was released in movie theaters and wartime food rationing began, a sullen Evelyn Almond was driven to Milwaukee and enrolled in St. Mary's Academy, a strict Catholic girls school.

Mom later described St. Mary's as a "convent," com-plaining she still had calluses on her knees from the inter-minable hours spent at prayer, supposedly begging forgiveness, though some must have been spent wishing for revenge against Charles Schmidt. Bitterly she recalled long periods when she was forbidden from uttering so much as a word. So traumatized was Mom that the day she graduated from the convent was the last day she practiced the Catholic religion. When Dad enrolled Cindy and Connie in that convent school, he couldn't have issued a bigger challenge to Mom about her daughters' futures.

Though Charles Schmidt lived until 1962, the year Jodie was born, I have no recollection of ever meeting him, and don't remember Mom even mentioning him. I think she saw him as a man who tried to break her spirit; he became the embodiment of everything she distrusted in men.

The Reverend Marvin Fitz, Lucy's pastor and friend for thirty-five years, on the other hand, remembers Schmidt as a "loving and gentle man." Fitz, who buried Lucy and her two husbands, recalled her marriage to Schmidt as happy and characterized by devotion. His long illness and death was a terrible blow to Lucy, though she retained her faith and cheerfully ministered to her husband's needs until the bitter end, according to the pastor.

I don't think Mom ever forgave Lucy for allowing Charlie Schmidt to force her to atone for her youthful sins. Trapped in St. Mary's, uninterested in religion, she had plenty of time and reason to nurture her resentment. Then her misery was compounded by devastating news. Her biological mother, Josie, never having recovered from the anguish of giving up her love child, had grown hugely obese, a situation compounded by an untreatable thyroid condition. Miserable, Josie committed suicide.

Jodie and I have always wondered if this story is true or if it was an excuse for Mom's own weight gain. It always seemed to us that the real cause was her love of fine food rather than genetics. But the tragic story of our biological grandmother's death served another purpose. Throughout our childhoods it made us all terrified we would get grossly fat and suicidal.

On graduation day, Mom knelt on cold concrete in penance for the last time and left St. Mary's Academy. That was the end of her formal education. Determined to make up for lost time, Mom went to nearby Chicago, where she sang in numerous jazz clubs, achieving a modest success. There she fell in love with and married a young navy man, also from Rockford. According to Mom, he was never home and was often away to his first love, "the sea." The pattern of men betraying Mom and failing her continued.

Following her divorce from her first husband, she and a friend named Gloria headed for California, hoping to start a new life. In Los Angeles she was unable to find work singing and was "too shy to take a stab at the movies," but landed a job in downtown L.A., working for the Bell Telephone Companies' Yellow Pages division.

She was far from ready to give up on men in uniform, though. When she met tall, gallant Air Force Lieutenant Colonel Lucius Fisher Foster III, it didn't matter that he already had one failed marriage and was the father of three children; it was love at first sight for them both. Dad remembered her years later, despite all the bitterness that came between them, as: "the most beautiful woman I had ever met. She was articulate, outspoken, everything I had ever wanted in a woman.

"We were introduced at a fencing meet. The master instructor told me Brandy had come to learn to fence. He begged me to talk her out of it."

Dad remembers that the boring phone company job she had drove Mom mad. One day when they were first dating, he picked her up at the end of the day and saw she still had a huge pile of papers to file. She took the lot and crammed them into an already overflowing drawer. The next day she was fired, which bothered her not at all.

Over New Year's weekend 1954, Dad convinced her to go

to Tijuana, Mexico, for a romantic holiday. While in Mexico, Lucius proposed and the love-smitten couple was married by a justice of the peace.

"I know we were married in Tijuana, but I can't remember a thing about it," laughs Dad. It's a comment that says much about his attitude during those days toward family and relationships.

Mom always described Dad's background, proudly, as "very Waspy." One of his forebears was an eighteenth-century New Yorker who had adamantly opposed the Revolution. His support for King George cost him his fortune, but following independence he soon made another. The gaining and losing of fortunes is a pattern that was repeated many times over by the Fosters during the succeeding two centuries.

Dad's great-grandfather was one of the original builders of the Hathaway Building in Chicago, part of the late nineteenth-century style known as the Chicago School of architecture. Lucius built his massive fortune by deforesting great swaths of lower Canada and the upper tier of America. Like a robber baron, he bought and merged twenty paper mills in New England and became the nation's chief producer of newsprint, boxes, paper bags, and wood, virtually cornering the market. The company he founded became International Paper.

It was a family empire that was not destined to last. "His wife, Alice Fisher—my grandmother—set out to spend all that money. It was a full-time job for her, but she got to be very good at it," says Dad. Alice's son, Lucius II, was the founder of the Cherry Hill Golf Club in Denver. He, too, is mostly remembered for spending money. Granddad passed away just a few years ago, well into his nineties, which was a bit of a miracle considering he was a severe alcoholic by the time was twenty-five. His wife, Constance, could match him drink for drink. Their son, Lucius III, was born April 16, 1922.

Despite the abandon with which he pursued it, my grandfather lacked the constitution for a lifetime as a drunk. He first sought help when he developed a severe stomach disorder. Fortunately, Alcoholics Anonymous, then a new treatment regimen, was starting a branch in Los Angeles. Granddad became one of the charter members and attended meetings sporadically throughout his life.

The event that finally sobered him up was horrifying. In the course of his days-long drunken benders, during which he threw away huge amounts of money, mostly on Hollywood "party girls" and hangers-on, Granddad cut a self-destructive path. After a particularly long and violent spree, he woke from a comalike stupor that had lasted two days, and found himself in bed with a dead woman.

The house was littered with shattered glass; dried blood was caked on both their bodies and trailed across the floor. Apparently Granddad had nestled next to her and fallen asleep thinking she had passed out. What he didn't know was she had taken a lethal overdose of barbiturates in addition to wildly excessive amounts of alcohol. The young woman died of heart failure during the course of the night.

When he finally regained consciousness, rigor mortis had set in and her body had started to decompose. The shock was sufficient to sober him up for good.

Incredibly, despite knowing how much his wife drank,

Grandfather Lucius left Dad in her care and moved out, never to return. Putting his failed marriage, as well as his young son, completely out of his mind, he moved back to Denver, where he continued to play golf and spend his father's money. Within a few years he was remarried and had a new family to replace the discarded one.

Constance, like her husband, was an alcoholic of the worst sort. When she was drinking, she drank day and night and was consumed by mood swings characterized by depression and rage. For many of his most formative years, Dad was subject to these nightmarish swings. By all accounts, his mother was often nasty and her behavior erratic. Grandma Connie was a woman who either got her way or bulldozed whoever was in it.

In the thirties, Constance drove a Pierce-Arrow, the American Rolls-Royce, with a sixteen-cylinder engine and a body nearly as large and powerful as a tank. One day Dad and Grandmom were cruising up the Pacific Coast Highway, which was then a narrow, unpaved, windy road, in the great car. They had spent the evening at a party, and Grandmom was well on her way to oblivion. Roaring along at a frightening speed, she paid no attention to an old Model T Ford sputtering and coughing toward them. Dad said resignedly, "We're going to hit that car."

Grandma ignored his warning and smashed into the other car with such force the Model T was reduced to little more than a pile of rubble on the side of the road. Not only did she not stop, Dad recalls she didn't even bother to look in the rearview mirror to see the havoc she had wreaked. The next morning the police appeared at the door to ask about the accident. Far from being contrite, Grandmom said: "I was far too drunk last night to recall any such accident."

Incredibly, the officer merely gave her a lecture on driving safety and left without arresting her or even writing a ticket. The only possible explanation was the substantial contributions Grandma made to police charities, including the Widows and Orphans fund. The money was obviously well spent.

Despite her drinking, Constance Foster managed to make a mark in Los Angeles. She was one of the first American women to learn to fly, using cold cash to overcome the reluctance of the shocked instructor she approached. In the midst of the Great Depression, Constance went to the thriving garment district east of downtown Los Angeles and opened a one-room sportswear business. Through hard work and good design skills she prospered. With her partner and boyfriend, Louis Gerst, a clothing manufacturer, she managed to turn her tiny enterprise into a multimillion-dollar clothing empire. The Constance Foster label was soon known around the world.

I remember Dad driving us past the site of her great home and pointing out where it once stood. The mansion had been a stately white Georgian house with a colonnade built on several lushly landscaped acres at 1012 Crescent Drive, behind the renowned Beverly Hills Hotel. She bought it in the thirties for $25,000—a steal. By the early fifties it was worth $150,000.

Sadly, despite her success she never gave up drinking. She spent many of her evenings at home wandering about with a cigarette in one hand and a bottle in the other. Her end came on October 25, 1954, appropriately enough with a blaze of glory that old-timers in Beverly Hills still talk about. She passed out with a lit cigarette in her hand, causing a fire that set her huge canopied bed aflame. The fire spread to the silk draperies and rapidly turned the bedroom into an inferno. Her huge mansion became a funeral pyre. Strong Santa Ana winds buffeting the city that night spread the blaze to other great houses nearby, endangering her whole Beverly Hills neighborhood. She was only 53.

During his life, Dad has rarely had more than a beer or two as a result of his horrifying youthful exposure to alcoholism. But with his usual stoicism, he has always refused to talk about the years he lived with his alcoholic mother on his own, other than to admit it was not pleasant. I have always thought his upbringing was a key to understanding his failings as a father and husband. When I complained about the way he left us, he said that his father did the same thing, as though one sin justifies the other.

On the positive side, Dad shared with his mother a passion for flying. Dad first flew when he was just five years old, in a tiny World War I–era plane called a Jenny. "I think I was born addicted to flying," he says.

Dad had a burning ambition from very early on to become a fighter pilot. His grandfather, noticing that among his progeny Dad alone seemed to have a spark of ambition, took an interest in him. During a short time when Dad lived on the Foster estate in Denver, he taught him how to make things with his hands and how to do construction work, the kind of labor other family members held in contempt. Dad proved an apt pupil, quickly learning the trade, which was a good thing, because once the family fortune was finally frittered away by others, he was forced to depend on those skills to survive.

Along with flying, the gentlemanly art of fencing became another obsession. He took private lessons from a master and spent endless hours practicing on his own. Though Dad is too self-effacing to say so, he might have won a place on the U.S. Olympic fencing team had the war years not intervened.

After high school, Dad accepted an offer of admission to Yale University, where Jodie would one day be an honors student. Just before the school year was to begin, he arrived in New Haven, Connecticut, at the two-hundred-fifty-year-old campus with its ivy-covered gothic buildings. He instantly found his fellow students insufferably stuffy; even the boys his age favored tweed jackets and smoked meerschaum pipes.

Before orientation was over, he fled, hitchhiking to New York City. His skill at swordsmanship won him recruitment to the more bohemian New York University, in the heart of Greenwich Village. There he began studying engineering and aeronautics, determined to accomplish his goal of being the best fighter pilot in the skies. After less than a year, war was roiling in Europe and he was determined to take part in the fighting as soon as possible.

Frustrated by America's stance of neutrality, Dad crossed the border to Canada, which had declared war on the Axis powers in 1939. Desperate for aerial fighters, the Royal Canadian Air Force instantly enrolled him in a training program. In no time, he was screaming through the skies in Fleet Finch and Tiger Moth war planes. Proudly wearing the bars of a first lieutenant, Dad sailed for England just in time to take part in the critical Battle of Britain, which raged in the skies over England during the fall of 1940.

When the United States joined the fighting in 1942, Dad was given amnesty for having renounced his U.S. citizenship and offered a commission with the U.S. Army 8th Air Force. He flew over a hundred missions, serving in both the European and Pacific theaters, and was one of the most highly decorated flyers in the air force.

Dad kept his many medals in a large box when I was a little boy. One day, presumably because I was angry about all the fighting in our house, I took the box outside and buried his precious war ribbons and awards in the yard. He exploded with rage, making the ultimate threat, which was to leave for good. The incident shows how clearly our father simply did not know how to be a father. He'd had no role model as a boy, only parents who abdicated their responsibilities. It left him unable to make connections with us while we were young and being raised by a woman who had the most bitter experiences with untrustworthy men. My sisters have never forgiven him for that abandonment; Jodie will not even speak to him.

Though I did grow closer to our father as time passed, I often found that, perhaps because he had been forced to be so self-sufficient as a child, he could not understand the lack of that quality in others. During his service in the Pacific, he was shot down behind enemy lines. Suffering excruciating pain from a broken back, he walked twenty miles and slept in a sewage ditch to escape capture. In the course of a long rehabilitation, Dad became addicted to morphine, which he claimed he kicked as easily as flicking a gnat off his arm.

Several times when I was suffering from my various

medical problems and addictions, Dad cited his soldierly strength as a model I should emulate. Of course, I promised to take his advice, but thought to myself, My God, I wish life was that easy. More than anything else in the world, I would have liked to have willed my dependency away that effortlessly.

I'm glad to say that Dad and I do talk, now that we're both wiser and more aware of the mistakes we've made. But this reflects lessons I learned long after my childhood, lessons that had to be learned despite being raised without my father. For Connie and Cindy and me, our childhood was always divided into the time with Dad and the time without Dad. For Jodie, there was only the time without Dad, the time with Aunt Jo.

Aunt Jo was born on October 9, 1930, in Tucson, Arizona. Her grandfather, whom I once met when Chris and I went to Arizona to visit his relatives, had fought alongside the legendary Mexican freedom fighter Emiliano Zapata. He was, of course, very old when I met him. But looking at his character-lined face, I saw where Jo got her strength and passionate sense of right and wrong, which she tried her best to pass on to all five of us children.

Shortly after Aunt Jo was born, her family moved to Los Angeles. After graduating from Beverly Hills High School in 1948, Jo enlisted in the Women's Army Corps. For most people, military service was an obligation they were happy not to have imposed on them or on members of their family. But Jo always had a strong sense of duty, and that, combined with the opportunity for education and travel the army offered a woman from a family of limited means, made her buck the national trend and sign up. (It makes me smile to consider that Mom's passion for soldiers in uniform found another outlet in her love for Aunt Jo.)

After her tour of duty was over, Jo found employment in the aviation industry that had taken root in the Los Angeles area during the war years, working first on the assembly line, then rising to become a quality control inspector. It gave her a steady, respectable income for a working woman in the 1950s.

She also married. I never met or even heard about Mr. Hill when I was a child, though I learned much from Chris later on. Mr. Hill and Jo had been good friends, and, while he loved her, he realized that she was simply not interested in men beyond having a child. The depth of his devotion to her was displayed by the fact that, though he moved to New York and started another family, he did not divorce Jo. In fact, he wrote to her every week, sending money to help support Chris. Jo herself never spoke about this arrangement, but I think that for a lesbian in the early 1960s who so clearly loved being a mother, it was a way to have a child of her own.

Helping to raise my sisters and me brought her great fulfillment, and she returned her happiness to our family. Over the years they were together, Jo lifted Mom out of brooding, gloomy moods many times. It was hard to be blue when she was around. She had a sharp sense of humor, could make jokes without putting anyone down. Whereas Mom and Dad had been at each other's throats without respite, Mom and Aunt Jo shared many of the same passions. They were both devoted cooks and often took us on train trips to Mexico for spices and herbs to concoct special meals.

Though there was never a lot of money, they rhapsodized over hard-sought bargains on fine wines.

Those trips to Mexico were particularly fun. Jo, though born and raised in the United States, spoke flawless Spanish, so we were able to find the small, bargain restaurants off the tourist path, where the food was wonderful and the prices right. Even as a little tyke Jodie picked up Spanish from Jo and wasn't shy about trying it out on our trips. I'll always remember Jodie at age five in Tijuana, wearing a huge sombrero that dwarfed her little head, with an ironic little smile on her face.

Quite unlike Mom, Jo never lost her temper, let alone screamed at the top of her lungs. When we misbehaved, Jo would sit down with us and calmly explain what we had done wrong and why we shouldn't repeat it. This was a kind of parenting my sisters and I had never known before. Jo became a buffer between us and Mom. When a tirade started, she would say, in a soft voice: "Just don't pay attention. She's had a very hard time in her life. Try to understand your mother."

Eventually, Mom turned almost all discipline and most basic child-rearing over to Aunt Jo, which was fine with us. Occasionally, Mom demanded that Jo spank me, a chore she reluctantly and rather halfheartedly carried out. She always warned me that I had ten minutes to prepare for a spanking. That time was used to throw on about ten pairs of underwear to cushion the blows. Aunt Jo pretended not to notice and doled out a few desultory swats with her bare hand. That satisfied Mom and was far better than facing her fury.

Jo wasn't perfect. She liked her tequila but never got

nasty from drink and seemed to overindulge only on the weekends. She was very family oriented in many ways. She often took us over to her sister Georgina's house in the Palisades section of Los Angeles. Georgina had a house that was always filled with divorced mothers who were trying to stick together and survive, so we fit right in.

We didn't have a conventional family with Aunt Jo, but that was never an issue for us. It took years before we realized the exact nature of Mom and Aunt Jo's relationship; I guess Dad's threats about unfit mothering made them cautious. Yet we understood that they were a pair; if a stranger had arrived to take one or the other of them out on a date, we would have known something was wrong. In moments of childhood crisis, for everything from scraped knees to attacks by a neighborhood bully, we had two mothers to turn to, one as comforting as the other. We cherished their relationship for everything it brought to our home. With Jo, we had the closest semblance to happy family life. It still wasn't *Ozzie and Harriet*, but it worked for us.

THREE

Strange, ugly things happen between single parents and children. And also the most beautiful things.   —JODIE FOSTER

As a baby just home from the hospital, Jodie had the lightest skin I had ever seen, and a perfectly bald head, save for a few little white hairs. From the beginning her eyes were deep, clear pools of blue. I would sit next to the crib and marvel at her.

About six months after Jodie was born, we moved out of the cramped duplex on Hamel Road, a house so filled with bad memories none of us missed it for a minute. Our new home was Aunt Jo's brand-new tract house in the Granada Hills section of the San Fernando Valley, finished to her specifications with advice from Mom. In the early sixties, that part of the valley was still mostly orange groves, and housing developments had just started to encroach. Our house fronted on a grove that stretched as far as the eye could see.

For city kids, marvels abounded. Just a short walk away was a wooden shack that looked like Jed Clampett's before the hillbillies moved to Beverly Hills. The man who lived there had an old dog that sat on the porch with him, and he carried a shotgun when walking through the groves. It was like glimpsing another world, one that had little time left in the San Fernando Valley, which would soon be covered, top to bottom, with concrete and condos. Compared with Hollywood, where we had always lived, it was heaven. All around us were uncompleted homes, which proved to be dangerous but wonderful fun.

One of the first treasures our new environment yielded was an ample supply of metal slugs that came in electric boxes. They worked great in candy machines and even came in nickel, dime, and quarter sizes. Another sport was climbing onto the roofs of the new houses and leaping into sand pits. To our alarm, Jodie could barely be restrained from constantly following in our footsteps.

Jodie stunned everybody, including her pediatrician, by learning to walk when she was only about six or seven months old, just after our move to Granada Hills. And at the end of her first year she spoke fluently, with an impressive vocabulary. She was precocious in every way, her curiosity and desire to learn unquenchable.

I do remember a tragedy that took place that year. Jodie's first birthday fell on a Tuesday, and Mom had plans to have some other mothers and their children over the following weekend to celebrate the happy day. But Friday was November, 22, 1963. John Kennedy's assassination changed the world forever and shattered Mom. Though I was only six, I remember how bereaved she was over the tragedy.

Mom had been a big Kennedy supporter and thought he was the best hope for the future.

It was mind-boggling how quickly Jodie developed in those years. She was simply the cutest, brightest kid around. Even as a small child Jodie had her now-famous husky voice. That voice, combined with some of the startlingly grown-up things she said, really amazed grown-ups. They would look at her quizzically, as though there must be something they had missed, like it was a trick. Jodie was fully aware of the effect she had on people and provoked it deliberately. She liked being thought of as extraordinary.

But she was also, in many ways, a typically rambunctious, pesky little sister. It was as though she was trying everything on for size; anything we did, she had to do, too. It was impossible for me to shake her, and she mimicked every-thing I said or did. If I said to Chris Hill, "Hey, Chris, when are we going to go out in the orange groves?" Jodie would repeat it. If I said, "Let's go get something to eat," she would repeat that, too. "Jodie, shut up," I'd snap, and she'd just flash that smile. It was hard to get mad at her with that smile of hers.

Because she walked and talked so early, we expected Jodie to do other things quickly as well. One of the few skills that didn't come early to her was potty training. There were no Pampers in those days, so she went around in cloth dia-pers, held together with pins and loaded with crap. And behind her would be Aunt Jo's little black cocker spaniel Tequila, sniffing at her butt. The Coppertone ad which made her famous could have been modeled on what she really was like as a toddler.

Despite allowing Aunt Jo to handle much of the daily

routine in the house, Mom was vigilant about seeing that we were "properly raised," a legacy, no doubt, from Lucy Schmidt. Cleanliness was a key part of that. She forced us all to march into the bathtub nightly and to wash our hands often. But Mom's campaign occasionally stopped short of diaper changing. Chris, who was the closest in age to Jodie, remembers: "Brandy did not like going near a dirty diaper. It was just understood that was my mom's job, and if she wasn't around, it sometimes didn't get done."

So from the time Aunt Jo left in the morning, Jodie was unchanged until Aunt Jo appeared again. She always seemed to have droopy diapers, a dirty face and hands. It was so bad when she was a toddler we called her Alicia Christina Cochina, Spanish slang for dirty Alicia Christina (Christina instead of Christian, because it rhymed with Cochina).

Partly to avoid Mom's cleanliness dragnet, Jodie developed a tremendous skill at escaping the house. She would slip away relentlessly. There was little Mom, Aunt Jo, or any of us could do to restrain her. Attempts to use childproof locks, door jams, and guard gates went for naught, because she figured out how to defeat them. She climbed through the doggie door, pried windows open, and pushed screens out. In retrospect, her feats were clearly a measure of her intelligence and precocity, but it was unnerving at the time. Every time I turned around there was smelly Jodie, with the dog at her rump and a peanut butter and jelly sandwich in her hand. (And she always had a pacifier in her mouth. Not until she was about four was she fully weaned from it.)

Aware of Jodie's skill as an escape artist, Mom was always afraid of her following us out in the orange groves, because she knew there were plenty of natural dangers. Chris and I, naturally, wanted to play with other boys our age, so we constantly tried to shoo her away, but had little luck. Having Jodie as a constant shadow was a hassle, because it meant I had the responsibility of looking after her.

The orange groves were full of spiders, tarantulas, and snakes. Once I captured a snake and showed Jodie the angry, hissing serpent up close, thinking it would convince her not to follow us anymore. But it had the opposite effect: she was fascinated and wanted to hold it.

Danger was meaningless to Jodie. She was driven by her inquisitiveness. Her fearlessness frightened us all, and for good reason. When Jodie was about nine months old, I was playing at my friend Eddie Maxwell's house. I was mad that she had succeeded in following me again, so Eddie and I were doing our best to ignore her. Suddenly I was struck by the sickening realization that something was wrong; I had no idea where she had gone. I called out Jodie's name, quietly, cautiously, at first. Then as a wave of panic swept over me, I shouted for her at the top of my lungs. Looking wild-eyed out the sliding doors at the pool area, my heart sank. Jodie was at the bottom of the pool. Eddie and I both jumped into the water. I was a fairly good swimmer, but I just couldn't get all the way to the bottom. I tried again and again, running out of breath and swallowing water, getting dangerously close to drowning myself. Finally, as I made one last lunge, I saw Eddie reach her, grab an arm, and head for the surface. He gently laid Jodie by the side of the pool.

We both looked at her and then at each other. I thought for sure she was dead. Her skin was blue and she didn't seem to be breathing at all. Reeling with horror, we knew there was something we were supposed to be doing, but neither of us moved to do whatever it was. Then Jodie gurgled from deep down in her lungs, coughed up a huge amount of water, and started crying. I cradled her in my arms and carried her home. Tears of joy that she had survived and horror at how close she had come to dying were streaming down both of our faces.

But the shock soon wore off. Los Angeles was full of public pools where children frolicked, and we were no exception. For months after the drowning incident, every time we visited our local pool, Mom kept a hand clasped on Jodie's wrist while the rest of us swam. It was torment for Jodie to watch us play without her, and she watched our every move. Then one day, inevitably, Jodie got free, and before Mom could grab her again, she darted straight to where we played in the water and plunged in.

There was a moment of shock before Mom could even scream. Then Jodie bobbed up, grinning like a maniac, and started to dog paddle.

The physical threats that Jodie encountered had fewer long-term consequences than the psychological turmoil that remained part of our life. In Granada Hills, the constant fighting between Mom and Dad was replaced by an ongoing struggle for the upper hand between mother and children. Eventually, Mom won only limited victories over her first three children, but succeeded completely with Jodie. In the process she instilled in us the strong and decent values she wanted. Unfortunately, she unconsciously passed along some less beneficial lessons as well.

Mom was dedicated to teaching us the basic Midwestern morals that had been drummed into her as a child. Her admonitions against lying, cheating, and stealing were the cornerstone of her child rearing. The fact that my sisters and I are incapable of deliberately unethical behavior toward others is something Mom considers one of her proudest accomplishments. In handling the tens of millions of dollars Hollywood throws her way, Jodie couldn't possibly pad the expenses and use creative accounting to bilk contributors to her projects out of their just rewards. Her sense of fair play makes her stand out in a city where scamming is not only condoned but expected.

Mom always demanded we behave perfectly and perform up to her exacting standards. She needed to be the most beautiful (and she was indeed a stunning woman) and the best dressed, to live in the finest home, and be the most successful person around. Anything less caused her terrible anguish. Though she did not embrace Lucy Schmidt's principles in many ways, she was still clearly her daughter.

The nonnegotiable demand that we be the best students, athletes, dressers, and the most well-mannered young ladies and gentlemen fell largely on deaf ears. At the time we didn't have the slightest understanding of Mom's motivation, so we fought her and added to her unhappiness and corresponding rage. In an interview Mom and I did together for *TV Guide* in 1970, she talked about how she yelled when she was angry: "I'm a screamer. When I go to bed some nights, I think the kids are living with a maniac."

Though Aunt Jo strove to be a moderating influence, fighting and rebellion were a way of life in our house. Confrontation had been the dominant aspect of Mom and Dad's relationship, and Cindy, Connie, and I had learned that it was an acceptable response to any situation we didn't like.

We taught that lesson to Jodie every day, and every time she escaped from the house or a bath, she proved how quickly she absorbed it.

But Cindy learned it best. From the time she was just five or six, even while our parents were still married, she frequently encouraged us all to run away from home. Because Dad's response to a fight with Mom was to leave and not come back for several days, Cindy assumed that was the thing to do. When Mom would punish her or refuse to let her have her way, she would run away. But it wasn't good enough for her to go alone, she needed to take all of Mom's kids with her to exact proper revenge. Many times she helped us to carefully put our little belongings in sacks tied to sticks. Off we marched through our neighborhood like a pack of midget hobos. Fifteen minutes later, frantic and screaming, Mom rounded us up and drove home.

While Connie, Jodie, Chris, and I had a mortal dread of Mom's wrath, Cindy seemed to relish running headlong into the lioness's jaws. While we shuddered, she would taunt her. Cindy picked up a range of Spanish vulgarisms, which she taught us and encouraged us to repeat in Mom's presence. If we ignored her, she beat us up. If we obeyed her, Mom was furious. The punishment for cursing was having Tabasco sauce dripped on the tongues of us older kids or our mouths washed out with soap. But most frequently misbehavior in any form was met with a sharp slap across the face, which was utterly demoralizing in addition to being painful.

In my memory, violence was always in our lives. Mom struck us older kids regularly. In our Ford Fairlane, Jodie sat in a child seat in front with Mom; Cindy, Connie, Chris, and I sat in the back. The rearview mirror was never focused toward the road behind us. Instead, it was tilted down so Mom could keep an eye on us. She was so short that we couldn't even see the top of her head from the backseat. But we could always see her vigilant eyes in the mirror. Fights over candy and a hundred other trivial things were constant. Mom tolerated a certain din, but no more. We would catch a glimpse of her eyes starting to blaze and know in a flash it was too late—we had crossed the line. Fast as a mongoose, she would strike, catching all of us with one smack. The blow was like a bowling ball, cleanly whacking every pin at once.

One of the worst, nearly disastrous, of these incidents happened when Mom became so enraged at Connie she chased her with a coat hanger and wound up accidentally hitting her in the face, near her eye. Fortunately, it was a lesson learned, because she never hit us with anything other than her hands after that—save for the occasional strap across the butt.

Violence was a behavior that once learned was very difficult to forget. Cindy beat on Connie, Connie pummelled me all the time, I took my frustration out on Chris, and Chris went after Jodie. Once, when nobody else was around, Chris dressed Jodie up in leather and shot at her with a BB gun. She never protested; it seemed like a perfectly natural thing to her. Jodie did often threaten to tell Mom when Connie and Cindy picked on Chris and me, though they usually managed to bribe or intimidate her into silence.

One of the continual sources of contention in our house was the lone bathroom. One day, convinced that Connie and Cindy were going to spend all day inside it, I began to shout for them to come out. They threw open the door and returned verbal fire, standard Foster family procedure. Jodie was sitting on the bed in the room she shared with Cindy and Connie, fascinated. I kept watching her out of the corner of my eye, convinced she was about to take sides with the enemy.

Then Mom appeared, her fury over yet another stupid fight more than a match for mine or the girls'. We had clearly pushed her as far as she could go that day; she was nearly in tears, despite her rage. "Go ahead, kill each other," she shouted in despair. "I don't care what you do."

Connie, Cindy, and I stood meekly aside as Mom fled to her bedroom, then watched in amazement as Jodie cautiously got off her bed and padded down the hall to Mom's room, where she curled up next to our sobbing mother. Whereas the rest of us caused Mom torment, Jodie offered comfort.

Though they would later have the normal parent-child conflicts over things like how Jodie dressed, Mom and her youngest daughter began to forge a relationship unlike any other in our house. It was as if Jodie had looked at her bizarre family and said, "There's nothing but grief in fighting Mom, and even if her standards are incredibly high, I can meet them, and maybe gain a little peace around here."

When Mom truly believes in something, she has always been resilient as well as relentless. After failing, in her mind, with her first three children, she found with delight that not only was her fourth with the program from the start, she was a fast learner who craved challenges. Like the rest of us, Mom showered attention on Jodie every time she mastered a new skill. Jodie realized that doing what she was told, and doing it exactly the way she was instructed, was the key to Mom's approval.

Mom took great satisfaction in Jodie's precociousness. The first time Aunt Jo took us to her sister Georgina's house, we older kids barged in like storm troopers, tearing up Georgina's living room rug with the roller skates we hadn't bothered to take off. Three-year-old Jodie padded in quietly beside an embarrassed Mom, who made a hasty round of introductions of her rowdy children. "And this is my daughter Jodie," she said finally. "She's quite a singer. Would you like to hear her sing? Sing something, Jodie."

Jodie grinned from ear to ear and burst into the first lines of the Herman's Hermits hit "Henry the Eighth" and then kept going through the whole song. None of us had taught it to her; she'd memorized it listening to the radio. There was no hesitation, none of the shyness that would have made most little kids blush and stammer. When she was through, she grinned again. Mom grinned even wider.

The perfectionism Mom insisted on led Jodie to attempt great heights, and it made her soldier on when most would have quit. But the psychic pain of always striving to climb a higher mountain is high. Since she was a little child, Jodie has been terrified of failure and always pushed herself far past any reasonable limits, whether it was in acting, school-work, or tennis.

By the time she was in grade school and her career had started, her low tolerance for failure was already showing. Sometimes a studio driver would have to pick her up from school and rush her to work. Jodie knew exactly what the shooting schedule was and what time she was meant to be on the set, when she was supposed to be getting her makeup and hair done, and what time she was expected to hit her mark before the camera. If the driver was late picking her up, or if they got stuck in traffic on the way, Jodie would have a fit, turning bright red and shaking uncontrollably. It was painful to see her go through such agony. Such were the consequences of failure in our house.

In addition to battles with the kids, Mom was often frustrated in her drive for the things she considered necessary to a good life. During the years we lived at Aunt Jo's, money was tight. Aunt Jo was struggling mightily to support us, but Mom passionately wanted to be independent and do more than make ends meet. She had a taste for art, gourmet food, and other fine things that were beginning to seem permanently out of reach. Her frustration and anger often reached the breaking point and seemed to turn in on her.

More than once I came home from school and found her on the living room floor in the fetal position, blue and shaking while Jodie looked on in terror. In an interview with the *Los Angeles Times* recently, Jodie talked about the distress she had felt when Mom collapsed like that. "Let's just imagine a scenario where your parent spends hours in the corner crying," she recalled sadly. "That is my great fear—to depend on somebody who is slipping away."

Seeing our mother in such a state made me feel terribly helpless. I vowed to myself that when I was a little older, I would find some way to help Mom out. Jodie responded the only way she knew how, by working even harder to be the little girl Mom wanted.

Aunt Jo continued to buoy us up. Though cash was

always in short supply, Jo was pretty imaginative about providing entertainment. Though we rarely took real vacations, there were many wonderful expeditions to Tijuana and occasional camping forays. Jo even managed to get us bleacher seats at Dodger baseball games once in a while.

The one activity we managed to afford regularly was going to the movies. Mom was a dedicated, obsessive fan. Most of the time we could only afford drive-ins, and even then Jodie and I had to hide under the seat to keep the admission price down. "Black top" theaters were plentiful in Los Angeles during the sixties. There was always a big playground in front of the screen, where we played until the show started at dusk. It wasn't just going to a movie; it was a picnic, a chance to run crazy with a pack of kids before we piled into the car again and hooked the tinny speaker over the open driver's window. So many of my childhood memories are set in our old Ford Fairlane station wagon, it seems like we lived in it.

On a trip to the San Diego Zoo in that station wagon, Jodie startled us all once again. "San Diego, twenty-seven," she announced. "Exit only." She was just three years old and already starting to read.

Mom beamed from ear to ear. She knew at that moment Jodie was destined for greatness at something.

Jodie was clearly a prodigy, and we all delighted in stimulating her mind. Connie read books to her every day, struggling to find stories that Jodie hadn't memorized. She could recite the complete works of Dr. Seuss before she was four. Cruising around Los Angeles in the Fairlane, we played the game of seeing who could spot license plates from the most states; Jodie always won. She had memorized the colors of so many states' license plates that she could make the call long before we were close enough to read the print.

We expected Jodie to do anything. She was in so many ways the perfect child to begin with—walking, talking, swimming, reading so early—it seems inevitable now that she would struggle to be the perfect actress, the perfect daughter. It was a reaction to the circumstances in our tumultuous house, but it was also the manifestation of an immense talent and will.

In Jodie's 1991 movie, *Little Man Tate*, a character describes Fred, the six-year-old genius whose mother Jodie plays, by saying in awe, "It's not just how much he knows; it's how much he *understands*." Understanding came early to Jodie, whether in reading or human relationships. She was never the social oddball child that Fred Tate is. She always had enough charm to win anybody over, and enough rowdy siblings to teach her the rough-and-tumble interaction skills kids demand of each other. Gregarious and an eager learner, Jodie absorbed everything that went on around her in the Foster family circus and the world at large. And all too soon the world was to learn just how precocious she was.

FOUR

I was raised to believe I was the great white hope. —JODIE FOSTER

As long as all seven of us were living on Aunt Jo's wages, I remained obsessed with finding some way to earn the money necessary to make us independent and our mother finally happy. My motivation for becoming a child actor was, at least in the beginning, purely to improve my family's lot. I believed that lack of money was the cause of our misery and of our mother's sometimes inexplicable behavior.

Out of the blue, a way presented itself. A neighbor in Granada Hills named Greg Shank was a child actor. He appeared on television and on billboards all the time, advertising Dippity-Do. He bragged that he had bought himself a cool mini-bike and already had money saved for college. There was no doubt in my mind I could do as well—and better. I begged Greg to tell me who his agent was and to introduce me. Oddly, he grew almost panicky at the idea and told me to get out of his house. Hearing the commotion, his mom came and asked what was going on. When I told her, she said I was cute and she would be glad to introduce me to Greg's agent, who happened to be coming to their house the very next day.

I was up at dawn the following morning, humming with anticipation. No one was going to keep me away from this agent. When we were introduced, I told her I was going to be the next big star and that she needed me. Far from being put off by my bluster, the agent was excited. It turned out I had the kind of attitude she was always looking for but seldom found. Unfortunately, she wasn't taking any newcomers, but said I was so promising she would recommend me to an agent who was also just starting out, Toni Kelman.

Mom was a little skeptical initially. She was very aware of how tough the entertainment business was; she knew how quickly stars rose and fell. Perhaps she remembered her own frustrated attempt to make it as a jazz singer as well. But she agreed to meet Toni, and a few days later Mom, Jodie, and I were on our way across the San Fernando Valley for an appointment.

Toni was still operating out of her garage at the time. Her son Rick had been a child actor, and she planned to use the knowledge gained managing his career to start her own agency. Toni was as excited and full of energy as I was; we were both determined to make it despite the steep odds, and Toni's enthusiasm won Mom over as well.

My first audition was at the advertising agency that handled S&H green stamps. Toni prepped me to have the same fired-up attitude I had shown the first agent, but she need not have worried. Giddy with anticipation, I came on like gangbusters. The ad people were used to children who were about as spirited as government mules, dragged to auditions by wanna-be stage mothers. I got the job.

The next audition was for Kellogg's cornflakes. I showed up with my own spoon and dug into the cereal bowl as though I was starving. From that point on I got every job I tried out for. I was so successful, mothers of other child actors sometimes turned and walked out in a huff when they saw me in the waiting room. Toni even sent me to jobs that called for a girl, or a child of a different age, because they often rewrote the script for me.

I credit my motivation for a great deal of my success, but I also have to say that Toni and her daughter Sandy helped me enormously. They stuck by me years later when I was going through the turmoil of my teens. Toni and Sandy were always there for me. Likewise, Toni was kind enough to credit me with helping her become one of the biggest youth agents in Hollywood. Once my career took off, so did Toni's; she moved from her garage to a suite of offices on Sunset Boulevard and never looked back. She later signed Barry Williams and many of the other Brady Bunch kids, and, of course, Jodie.

Toni nurtured Jodie and me as children who appeared to be worldly and professional, but who had egos and sensitivities that could be crushed in a second. Unfortunately, few people in the business possessed her kindness and perception.

In the meantime, the financial difference of having an actor in the family was tremendous. As soon as the money started to come in, Mom began house hunting, and soon settled on a place by the ocean in Newport Beach. We had lived in the area briefly when Dad was still with us, and Mom remembered it as a classy place where old-money Angelenos lived.

Sadly, Jo and Chris did not move along with us. The money I was making meant that for the first time in years Mom was not dependent on her partner. She was eager to start living the respectable life for which she had so long yearned. Aunt Jo, on the other hand, was committed to the house into which she had put her savings and was unwilling to leave it. Their paths began to diverge, yet Aunt Jo and Mom remained a couple, and Jo's house in Granada Hills was an all-purpose child-care facility where one or all of us would be deposited as our schedules grew more hectic.

I was too young to notice the signal change that the move would have on the relationship between Mom and Aunt Jo. This woman who had been a mother receded from our lives over the succeeding years, though it happened gradually. For the older kids, the thought of what amounted to a second divorce was too terrifying to contemplate, and we avoided noticing it. But Jodie did. Without Jo around to exert her pacifying influence, the fights between kids, and the fights between kids and parent, escalated. During one particularly wild exchange Mom collapsed on the couch, moaning in despair over how she would ever handle us. Cindy, Connie, and I kept right on yelling—until, with a stamp of her foot, four-year-old Jodie let out a plaintive howl: "I want Jo!"

Mom's moans turned to sobs at that comment, and we all saw how far we had drifted apart.

Accustomed as we were to fighting among ourselves, we

took the new level of warfare in stride—things weren't any worse in that respect, just more like what they always had been. But in other ways, Newport Beach proved to be as dramatic a change as Granada Hills and the orange groves had been. We all started surfing and spending days on the beach, which was something none of us had ever done before. My sisters and I became beach-blond, tanned sun worshipers. We had the freedom to roam up and down the strand at all hours, meeting the colorful characters that composed California beach culture in the sixties. You could meet a band of hippies, who lived like latter-day gypsies, then turn and wave to John Wayne, who lived on nearby Balboa Island, frequently sailed by, and attended church across the street from us. Mom began decorating the house with her usual panache, sun-bathed nude on our private deck, and for a time seemed happier than ever.

Apparently things were also looking up for Dad. When I was ten, I remember, he came by one day and showed off a bulging billfold of hundred and even five hundred dollar bills. He peeled off a couple of the big bills and gave them to Mom, then drove off. But mostly, very little aid was forthcoming.

Dad always blamed the lack of support on his assertion he was a poor businessman and seemed to come up short at the end of the week. All his life he has continued the Foster tradition of making and losing fortunes. He was either rolling in money or broke. Observing his highs and lows ultimately made all of us want to be cautious and responsible with our money, so as not to follow in his footsteps.

I was thrilled to see Dad, but I was the only one in the house who felt that way. In theory, he had visitation rights, but our contact was infrequent. At times Mom would tell me that he would be coming by on the weekend to pick us up, and I would sit on the front porch for hours waiting for him to arrive. When the appointed hour was finally long past, Mom would call me inside and say, "Buddy, you just have to pretend he's dead."

The bitterness between Mom and Dad went unabated for years, and Mom freely vented her anger over his behavior in our presence, cursing his unfaithfulness long after they were divorced, reminding us all that our reduced circumstances—even when they were on the upswing—were his fault. Perhaps the bond that was growing between Mom and Jodie made Jodie especially attuned to the message of Dad's failure. A long time ago, she decided Dad doesn't exist as far as she is concerned, so when she sees him in the flesh, it's very upsetting for her.

Incredibly, as big as Los Angeles is, they keep running into each other. When *Little Man Tate* premiered, Jodie invited students in California's program for gifted children to display their school projects at an exhibition she organized. Ironically, Luchan, one of Dad's school-age daughters by his current marriage, was in the program and was invited to the premiere. Jodie went from child to child examining their projects, commenting on them and offering encouragement. It was all done with her usual charm and poise, until she came to Dad and his daughter. She was, very uncharacteristically, speechless and flustered. Dad, with his customary savoir faire, tried to smooth the situation over and introduce Jodie to her half-sister, who was obviously excited to meet her. Jodie would have none of it. She smiled icily and moved on.

Dad has three children by his marriage prior to Mom, two school-age children by his current wife, a daughter who was apparently conceived in Korea during the war, and another girl whose genesis he hasn't explained. That was the only occasion when Jodie spoke to any of her seven step-siblings.

If Jodie learned that Dad was a failure, she also realized how a successful child could satisfy a parent. Mom was energized during the Newport years, exuding optimism and hope. She went to work with a vengeance, turning us into the upper-crust kids she wanted us to be. There were sailing lessons, cotillion dance lessons, instruction on everything from how to tie a tie to dinner table etiquette. Despite the flurry of tutelage, we all loved Newport.

Jodie and I did our first bit of acting together, of a sort, while we lived at the beach. At Christmas I asked Santa, very specifically, for a Ludwig snare drum. When I opened my drums Christmas morning, I was thrilled. Jodie and I decided we were going to imitate the Beatles. We got Beatles wigs and formed a little band. Jodie was George, Chris Hill was Paul, Georgina's son Larry Bowerline was John, and I was Ringo. Jodie looked priceless in a Beatles wig.

With a nice house in fashionable Newport and enough money to buy the furniture she had always wanted, I was sure that I had accomplished the impossible; Mom would finally be happy. Finally everything would be great. But somehow it wasn't enough.

Mom's dreams of independence started to become lavish. My agent, Toni Kelman, recalled, "We constantly got phone calls at the agency from creditors who were after her about bills. Her fur coat and diamond ring were often in and out of the pawnshop, and Brandy habitually came to me for loans.

"But her extravagance knew no bounds. I was incredulous when she bought a huge Lucite bed that I remember costing thousands of dollars.

"The one thing I could count on when she needed money was that almost no movie project for Buddy or Jodie would be turned down."

The turmoil continued, only at another level. Jodie and I came home from the beach one day to find Mom lying facedown on the kitchen floor, moaning about money: "How are we going to survive?" We didn't have the faintest idea what to do. Jodie got hysterical and began to wail, but it didn't seem to penetrate Mom's state. I asked Mom if she wanted me to get Mrs. Johnson, our neighbor, but got no answer. "Mom, Mom, what should I do?" I cried.

We had hoped that we had left the roller-coaster rides behind in Granada Hills, but they were still with us. I wondered if other kids went through such traumas, if other kids' mothers lay down on the kitchen floor and wept. I didn't think so even then, yet I certainly don't blame Mom. This was her way of coping with our problems. She fought and fought for us, and when all the energy was gone, she collapsed like a rag doll.

But negative experiences have a staying power that can overwhelm the memory of more mundane, happier hours. Jodie's recollection of her childhood is distinctly colored by incidents like the one above: "I was raised by my two older sisters and my brother. My mother had had enough," she told the *Philadelphia Inquirer* in 1994. It's an ironic comment given how closely Mom was involved in her career, but it indicates how much she felt that she, like the rest of us, was on her own.

The responsibility of pulling our weight in our household was always clear. About two months after Christmas, I came home and found my drums were gone; I was terribly confused. When I demanded to know what had happened, Mom said I hadn't played them enough and that they had been repossessed. I doubted that was the reason. I went to my room in tears, sorry that my drums were gone, but crushed that I wasn't properly supporting my family yet. We were, apparently, still in dire financial straits.

If I knew it, so did Jodie. From the beginning of my career, Jodie was curious about what I was doing. That shrewd, analytical mind of hers was constantly whirring, even though she was only four years old. I can't say that she set out at that age to earn her keep, but it was clear that my acting career was the center of life in our house, and that it made Mom happy. In retrospect, I should have realized that Jodie wanted a chance to shine, too.

Her first break came when I was auditioning for a Coppertone suntan lotion ad when I was nine. As usual, Jodie and Mom were in the waiting room. The casting directors asked me to take off my shirt because the shot they wanted required perfect skin pigmentation. The moment I stripped off my shirt, they started to laugh, which of course made me embarrassed and hurt. I couldn't understand why they were laughing at me. But when I turned around, I saw Jodie had wandered into the office. Barely out of diapers, she was wearing little ruffled shorts and had no shirt on.

Once she had their attention, she really put on a show, flexing her muscles and going through a repertoire of poses.

I yelled for Mom and tried to shoo her away. "Get your little ass out of here," I hissed.

But it was already too late. The casting agents were enchanted. When they asked her name, without hesitating she said: "Alexander the Great." They immediately decided Jodie was their model. They apologized to me and showed me out of the room. I was in a state of shock. Just like that, my little sister had muscled me out of a job, and soon she was grinning out of television sets around the country. The ad was so effective that even today Jodie is thought of as the Coppertone girl, even though the original image of a blond youngster in pigtails being pestered by a little dog was created thirty years before she was born.

I was furious at the time, but it quickly passed. While Jodie joined me as a breadwinner, for the time being my career was the engine that drove our family's finances.

That same year, 1966, I was offered my first costarring role in a TV series pilot. It was a Western called *Hondo*, in which I played a frontier widow's son, acting alongside Ralph Taeger, Kathie Brown, and Noah Berry, Jr. ABC television executives liked the pilot, which we filmed in the summer of 1966, and gave the green light for the series to shoot at MGM studios in Culver City.

Although my entire family was over the moon at this leap into regular television work, we also realized we were going to have to abandon our idyllic life on the beach. It was simply too far away from the studio. While we lived in Newport Beach, we had to rise before dawn to make the hour plus drive up the coast for early morning cast calls. Since Aunt Jo was no longer living with us, Mom had no choice but to bundle Jodie up and take her either to her friend

Delores Planting's house or to Aunt Jo's, then take me to work. I slept in the back of the car, but it was a grind for me and it must have been even worse for Mom.

Moving back to the city, though convenient, was a drag. Our new home, which we were promised would only be temporary, was a duplex apartment in Hollywood across from the Farmers' Market. We had the second floor of a 1930s Spanish mission-style house.

Jodie started kindergarten that year at the Hancock Park School, which was just down the street. Mom suffered from typical separation anxiety, watching little Jodie march off to school for the first time. It was months before she finally got comfortable with the idea of letting her go alone. But Jodie was adamant about not wanting to be driven to school or picked up afterward. She saw that the other little boys and girls walked, so she insisted she would as well. That was one of the first battles of will between Jodie and Mom, one that Jodie eventually won.

I remember that first day of kindergarten started off as the most exciting day of Jodie's life. Finally she would have a chance to do what the big kids did, reading and writing and all those books. Instead, she discovered to her disappointment and frustration that kindergarten stressed socialization skills, cutting and pasting, and learning ABCs. As little as she was, Jodie confronted her teacher and demanded she be given some sort of homework involving books. The teacher patiently tried to explain that she was the only student in the class who could read and she would have to wait another year before books were used.

"I'm not going back," Jodie announced when she got home that afternoon. "The other kids are babies! I don't want to learn to take naps and have somebody read to me. I don't like kids my age. I like older kids who are not so retarded."

As much as she was frustrated by the lack of challenge in school, Jodie could be maddening to adults when she was that age because she didn't fit the expectations they had for a child. For the most part she was already too much of a grown-up for them: Barbie dolls were anathema to her, she had no interest in fairy tales, hated jewelry and dresses. One of her favorite games was pretending she was James Bond, which she played all the time with Chris.

But the school took notice of her nimble mind and got over their surprise at her grown-up demands. Eventually they gave Jodie a battery of tests, and concluded she should be skipped to first grade. Jodie scored very high in all academic categories, and the teachers wanted Mom to consider enrolling her in a state-run science program for gifted children. Mom was vehemently against it and insisted Jodie stay where she was. That battle was won by Mom, who put her foot down and wouldn't entertain any arguments to the contrary.

In retrospect, it's hard to understand that decision, except for the fact that Mom had just agreed to have me held back a year. I was repeating the fourth grade, she told me, because I was so short for my age that I was sure to take a lot of abuse in a tough new school. I didn't buy it, and I was furious, and I wonder if Mom was simply trying not to rub salt in my wounds by advancing Jodie a grade.

She was already convinced that Jodie was going to flourish on her own anyway. Jodie once recalled sitting under a lemon tree as Mom told her how lucky she was to be a young woman in the 1960s, because she was going to be able to do whatever she wanted in life. She could be a doctor, a lawyer, an astronaut if she applied herself. Even then Jodie sensed a wistfulness to Mom's optimistic vision, because Mom never had a chance to be any of the things she had longed to be as a young woman. Yet, as young as she was, Jodie had no doubt Mom was right, that her life was going to be very, very different. That was a conviction Mom and Jodie shared and nurtured throughout Jodie's childhood.

Oddly, Mom didn't envision Jodie ending up as an actress. That was merely a short-range plan. Mom reminded us again and again in those years of the volatility of show business, and in urging Jodie and me to do well in school, she sounded the theme that actors as a lot were dumb and lazy. She was determined to see that we were neither. When our careers fizzled, she wanted us to be well-rounded people with an education to fall back on.

Mom wanted to refine us in other ways as well. We went to the Descanso Gardens in La Canada, to the Los Angeles County Art Museum, the Pasadena Museum, and once in a while out to the Getty in Malibu, where Jodie was fascinated by the Greek and Roman antiquities. We paid visits to the Griffith Park Observatory and to the planetarium to learn about the solar system. Mom had a real talent for entertaining us and exciting our hunger for knowledge.

Mom's sense of values extended to the public realm as well. She was a strong advocate of religious tolerance as well as civil rights, a legacy perhaps of her run-in with Charlie Schmidt over the issue of her liaison with a black man. During the sixties we marched as a family in numerous civil rights demonstrations, singing "We Shall Overcome," often in such tension-charged areas as South Central Los Angeles. Jodie and I walked until our legs gave out; then we were carried and, finally, put in cars that drove children to the end of the march, where we waited for our parents.

Given the volatility of the time, it might have seemed foolhardy for a couple of blond-headed children to be walking those mean streets, carrying placards and singing, but we detected no animosity or resentment. On the contrary, there was nothing but a kindred spirit for the cause of social justice. The riots that rocked Watts and later the whole country were a shock to us, but they didn't dim the belief Mom instilled in us about the importance of social change. Years later Jodie wrote: "Even the most shameful acts can reflect deep-rooted longings, a human face that we all share inside that gets confused somewhere along the way."

Jodie was just six years old in 1968 when one tragedy after another struck America, but she followed the events in the news as closely, and with as much comprehension, as most adults. Dr. Martin Luther King, Jr., was a greatly admired figure in our lives, a person we saw as a shining beacon of truth and a force for good. His assassination in April of that year had a devastating effect on us. It seemed like the end of all hope for a brighter future; all the things we believed in were shattered with one rifle shot.

But we felt all would not be lost if only Bobby Kennedy could be elected president. To our delight he won the California presidential primary election in June and was likely to be the Democratic nominee. Just a few miles from us down Wilshire Boulevard at the Ambassador Hotel, Bobby, his family, and followers celebrated the victory.

We had just gone to bed with the happy thought that Kennedy would lead our country out of Vietnam and bring racial peace, when Mom, sobbing with grief, woke us and tried to explain what had happened. The news that he had been shot just minutes before was too awful for us to believe, too numbing to comprehend.

In the days that followed both assassinations, Jodie was glued to the small black-and-white television in Mom's bedroom, watching the heartbreaking eulogies, the weeping widows, and the solemn funerals. In fact, during Jodie's most impressionable years, through the late sixties and early seventies, an appalling cavalcade of violence and hatred played out on our little TV screen and in the streets of America. Slaughter in Vietnam was on our television every night, eclipsed only by paroxysms like the Manson murders that took place in the hills near us, the shooting of four unarmed antiwar students at Kent State University, and a police riot at the 1968 Democratic convention in Chicago.

Those events had a lasting impact on forming Jodie's worldview. She finds violence abhorrent but fascinating, refuses to watch, let alone participate, in a movie about war, and she has a certain cynicism about the permanence of life and people. Attachments invite disappointment, which inevitably comes when the people one loves suddenly are snatched away. Yet she absorbed from Mom the importance of making a statement in spite of frustration and disappointment. She still sometimes wears a reversible pendant with portraits of Martin Luther King, Jr., and Robert Kennedy.

In the meantime, Mom was dedicated to making our careers work. Toni Kelman remembers, "From the very beginning Brandy pushed to get Jodie working full-time.

When Jodie first signed with me, Brandy called up complaining that she wasn't working enough. 'I guess you just don't like my daughter,' she said accusatively. 'She's only six!' I said, somewhat astonished."

But Mom kept up her campaign to launch Jodie, telling Toni that if she didn't line up more work for Jodie, Mom would take both of us to another agency. Since I was by far Toni's biggest client, Mom was really using the heavy artillery there.

Even Connie got in on the act briefly, doing a photo shoot for Catalina sportswear. But her heart wasn't in it, and she didn't throw herself into auditions the way Jodie and I did, so the Catalina job was the end of her modelling career. Jodie, meanwhile, went from the Coppertone ad to Nabisco's new national campaign for Oreos, to a commercial for Ken-L-Ration dog food (with me) and a spot for Crest.

Hondo lasted only half a season, from September to December 1967, despite fairly respectable ratings, but much good came from it. It was a great showcase and attracted a lot of interest. And I discovered one of the all-time legends of show business was a fan of mine, when Elvis Presley, whom I held in awe, dropped by the set.

Elvis was filming his movie *Speedway* on the MGM lot at the same time we were shooting *Hondo*. One day he came over to the set. Modestly introducing himself, as though anyone alive wouldn't have known who he was, Elvis drawled, "I'd just like to say I'm a big fan of the show, Buddy." I was absolutely blown away.

Another series shooting at the time was *Please Don't Eat the Daisies*. A remarkably well-trained, lovable English sheepdog was a regular on the show, and I fell in love with her. To my delight, the dog had puppies, and Mom bought one of them for me, which I named Hondo. Hondo turned out to be just as lovable as his mother. When the dog grew to full size, which was enormous, Jodie climbed on his back as though he was a horse, held his fur like a mane, and rode around the block with me leading. We became a little sideshow in the community. People would laugh and applaud as we strolled the streets.

But like the Ludwig snare drums, Hondo disappeared one day. On the awful afternoon we came home from school and learned our dog had been given away, Mom curtly told us we had failed to live up to our responsibility of cleaning up after our animal and taking care of him. There had been no warning, that I remember, or second chance. We were inconsolable. Jodie and I grieved, shrieked, and finally prostrated ourselves, all in vain.

These sudden changes, this invocation of standards that we hadn't known existed, taught us all that we had to perform at the top of our game all the time, and that even then happiness wasn't certain. It was a perfect preparation for life in Hollywood.

Fortunately, Jodie's awesome talent and dedication quickly began to pay dividends, thanks largely to astute decisions on Mom's part. But though Jodie was established in the next few years as one of the most successful child actors around, this period also brought a rapid fraying of our already conflicted family relationships.

One of the most stinging, and sadly final, things Jodie ever said to me was: "We never had a family and never will," and that I needed to "get over" trying to bring our family together for anything other than awkward, stilted, twice-a-year gatherings. Those words were spoken during a dark time in both our lives. I was a wreck, grasping at straws for stability, and Jodie was already the target of John Hinckley, Jr. Since then Jodie has learned a great deal about the importance of family relationships. But the words reflect the extent to which she was frustrated by the bizarre way of living in our house.

Jodie, armed with her prodigious talent, was learning to be a professional, investing her energy in acting, doing her best to stay clear of the chaos at home. It wasn't that she avoided us or disliked us, but that she resolved that though all the fighting was inescapable, she would simply have to do what she wanted despite it.

It was perfect preparation for the grueling work that lay ahead of her.

FIVE

On the West Coast, if you have problems, you don't talk about them. You go to the beach. —JODIE FOSTER

During the winter of 1967–68, I landed my first role in a feature film, *Angel in My Pocket*, costarring Andy Griffith and Jerry Van Dyke. It was a good family film that got some decent notices. But the most important benefit was that Griffith liked my work and recommended me for the spin-off of his hit series *The Andy Griffith Show*, of which he had grown weary after eight years. *Mayberry, R.F.D.* retained the *Griffith Show* cast except for Ron Howard and Andy. Ken Berry played a widower, just as Andy had in the original. I took over the Ron Howard role as his son. Aunt Bee, played by the delightful Frances Bavier, who was just like her character, moved in with us.

Despite some initial skepticism at CBS that the show would not retain its audience without the stars, *Mayberry* was an instant hit when it debuted in the fall of 1968, and quickly climbed to number three in the Nielsen ratings, lasting for four full seasons and seventy-eight episodes.

Mayberry was a great set to grow up on. Ken Berry was terrific, and Frances Bavier was like a kindly grandma. The only incongruous note was the peculiar smell of burning leaves that always seemed to be wafting from the trailer of one of the cast members. Years later, I realized the smell was marijuana smoke.

Jodie made her TV series debut on the show, playing a ballerina in a school play of *Sleeping Beauty*. It was a tiny walk-on role, and no one took any notice of her except for me. I saw that glint in her eyes during those brief seconds she was before the cameras. There was no doubt in my mind or Jodie's. That child was determined to be a star.

From the very beginning Jodie had the ability to hit the mark and get her scene right on the first take. Seeing her do it every time was a source of frustration, as well as admiration, because I always needed several tries. She also had a photographic memory. After one reading, the most complicated script was committed to memory.

Jodie and I studied acting with Lois Aour, who was one of the top acting coaches in Hollywood. Memorization was not my strong point, and Lois drilled me on it, while with Jodie she concentrated on cold reading and method acting. Ironically, Jodie was so much the little adult that she had to work with Lois to develop the range of responses that were expected of little kids: Jodie had to learn to act like a child. We went to Lois for years, three times a week, for three hours, working through each new script. She had a large impact on my career and certainly on Jodie's. It's been said that Jodie had no formal training in acting, but that's not true at all and fails to give Lois the credit she deserves.

Admittedly, Jodie soon found her own way. Her approach to acting became almost Zen-like. She is now completely the opposite of a method actor. It takes her a mere second to get into character. She just relaxes and flows into it. I don't think it's something she could explain or teach to other people. I've heard her compare acting to archery, drawing comparisons to how archers can "become one with the target."

Even though Jodie breezed in behind me and got her first advertising job with ease, her career came harder than mine: she had many more ups and downs, and she took it much more seriously. Of course, she lasted much longer. As an adult she recalled her first years in the business with more ambivalence than I felt toward my beginning: "I remember being in commercials and doing them over and over again, having to eat sickening things all day and throwing up. After being in a shampoo ad, I couldn't get the shit out of my hair for ten days.

"But there were people on those sets who were like my family—a misfit family of people who did not lead conventional lives. They played with me, but they also reprimanded me when I got bratty."

At seven years old Jodie landed her first series job on *The Courtship of Eddie's Father*, which lasted three seasons, from 1970 to 1972. The star of the ABC show was Bill Bixby, a widower who had a comedy-of-errors date each episode with different women his son, Eddie (Brandon Cruz), set him up with in hopes of getting a new mom. Jodie played

Joey Kelly, a tomboy schoolmate of Eddie's who seemed to beat him up most weeks.

Unfortunately, *Mayberry R.F.D.* was shot at the Desilu studios in Hollywood, where *I Love Lucy* had been made, and later at the Warner Brothers studio in the valley. *Courtship* was shot at the MGM studios in Culver City, so Mom had to run all over Los Angeles whenever Jodie was working. Even then the traffic was horrendous, so when we both had jobs, she was one busy woman. She became extraordinarily adept at juggling things, dropping one of us off at Aunt Jo's, taking the other to a set, going back to pick up the other, then making another cast call on the other side of town.

At our studios, Jodie and I both quickly became part of the family, learning who were the kindly directors, costumers, and technical people, as well as who were the W. C. Fields types, who chomped cigars and said, "Get outta here, kid. Ya bother me." After a mistake or two, we learned nobody was terribly long on patience. Big money, egos, and careers were on the line with each passing minute of shooting time, and being a kid was no excuse for screwing up.

On days when things weren't going well, it was sheer agony. We wished more than anything we were just normal kids with nothing more than schoolwork and playground bullies to worry about. Studio bullies were much more frightening than anything in school.

Years later Jodie recalled ruefully: "As a child I was yelled at more than other people, and it would always be my fault. I learned that to be professional was the number-one priority. If your dog dies, if your child has leukemia, it's no excuse."

In early 1969, shortly after it became obvious *Mayberry* was going to be a hit, Mom went shopping for a new house. The day she took us all to look at the one she had chosen for the first time, I was stunned. It was a white stucco, mission-style home on Cahuenga Terrace in the Hollywood Hills. A large picture window overlooked the Hollywood Bowl. The backyard had a waterfall and pond with a stone lion spitting streams of water. Jodie, Chris, and I would build a tree house there.

With my income, as well as Jodie's, Mom was finally able to carry out her dream decorating and furnishing job. During the week after we moved in, trucks pulled up and unloaded every few hours, disgorging eighteenth-century French armoires, lavish tapestries, zebra skin rugs, and copper pots for the kitchen. Mom scoured local antique shops and filled the new house with them, artfully mixed with contemporary works by artists like Andy Warhol. In the end the house was ready for the pages of *Architectural Digest*.

Once Mom was finished decorating, she announced a new policy: children were not allowed to play anywhere but in our own rooms or outside. We were all but banned from our own house. Mom told us she needed space to be alone. She said that being an only child, she wasn't used to being around other people all the time, and she needed a place to read her books on architecture and interior design in peace. I knew that we could get on her nerves with our constant fighting, but it seemed rather ironic that we weren't allowed to touch things purchased with our salaries. (I also thought it was odd when I found that Mom had credit cards and a bank account in my name, though she assured me that they were simply for professional expenses.)

Jodie says she never had a problem with Mom's attitude about putting much of the house off limits to us and guarding her privacy so closely. I guess that is one of the essential differences in our personalities: I like to be with the family, to run with the pack. Mom and Jodie feel completely the opposite way. Their "space" is most important. "One of the things that worked well with my mom was that we left each other alone," Jodie said as an adult. "We could be alone together."

All of our lives changed radically that year, but Mom's most of all. She went to Germany and checked into a world-renowned spa where she was given every kind of mud bath, massage, and renewal therapy available, and—most important—lost weight. When she returned, glowing with health, we hardly recognized our own mother. She had shed so many pounds, she seemed a different person, twenty years younger and svelte for the first time in years.

Traveling often to Europe, Mom became enchanted with France and decided to buy a chateau there. But after shopping around, she settled on a flat in Paris. Mom was enjoying the trappings of the good life as never before. She started frequenting the finest restaurants in Los Angeles—where she gained back much of her lost weight—and became more selective about her companions.

Toni Kelman, who was my agent and Jodie's until 1976, had become Mom's friend and often traveled with her. She recalled one trip in particular: "At our hotel in Spain, Brandy laid out her new clothes in the room with all the price tags still in place. When I asked her why she didn't remove them, Brandy said, 'Because I want people to know I'm a woman of class, that I buy expensive clothes.' "

One of the most unexpected changes in Mom's lifestyle came in that year of 1969, when she announced she had fallen in love and planned to marry. Her fiancé was a handsome, rugged studio technician on the *Mayberry* set named Frank Miller, who roared up to the house on a huge Triumph motorcycle. My sisters and I just stood and stared at each other in wonderment, while Mom beamed.

During their courtship everything was kept very proper, in accordance with Mom's peculiar sense of moral right and wrong. Several times over the years she piously pointed out that she had never had a man sleep over, and even her fiancé was no exception. But he did come to visit almost every morning for breakfast and more than won my approval by taking me to school on the back of his Triumph. Arriving at school on the motorcycle did more for my popularity than all my film and TV appearances.

Jodie remained somewhat frosty to Frank Miller. When I raved about the Triumph, she regarded me askance and said, "There are other things that make men cool, Buddy." Years later, she said in an interview that she felt that her own relationship with Mom was such that she was a "replacement for a husband," an odd statement that made even Mom somewhat uncomfortable, though I think it reflected the responsibility Jodie felt toward Mom and her happiness. At the time Mom wasn't sure Jodie would accept her getting remarried, saying, "At least I'm hopeful she will."

When the time came for Mom and her beau to thunder off to a Las Vegas wedding chapel, I was ecstatic, telling all my friends that I was finally about to get a new, hip dad. But it wasn't to be. Mom and Frank called us together and said they had simply decided the marriage wouldn't be right.

They abruptly stopped seeing each other, and the matter was over as far as Mom was concerned.

At the time the reason for the breakup remained a mystery to us kids. I wondered if Mom was trying to love a man again but couldn't, or perhaps knowing how happy I was when Frank was around, she just did it in an attempt to please me. Typically for our family, the matter was never discussed again. Instead we collectively pretended it never happened.

Many years later I learned that the episode was part of a larger cataclysm. Aunt Jo was already becoming less and less of a force in our lives at the time. It seemed we never had time to see her. Mom and Jodie were often away, and Cindy, Connie, and I were more interested in running wild than in turning to another parental figure. Chris Hill told me Jo resented being shunted aside as our fortunes increased, and to a degree Aunt Jo felt she had been used. But the most painful aspect for her was being separated from the children she felt she had raised.

Apparently, according to Chris and other members of Jo's family, what finally destroyed the relationship was a slip of the tongue. Aunt Jo's sister Georgina knew a close friend of Frank Miller's and was floored when he announced Frank was planning to marry Brandy Foster. She blurted out that she thought her sister and Mom were still an item. Word got back to Frank that Mom was having a lesbian relationship, and a few days later came the announcement that the wedding was off.

Filled with rage over what she saw as a betrayal, Mom blamed Jo and told her she was out of our lives forever. She also accused Jo of stealing from her, both to her face and within our hearing. I couldn't believe it, and I continued to see Jo on my own, though Jodie, always tightly in orbit around Mom, had no chance.

Sadly, after the split Jo was never quite the same person. She floundered, according to Chris and her family, and wasn't able to find a purpose again. She, like me, was the kind of person who couldn't be fulfilled without family around. One of the last times I saw her was during a period when I was living at the beach in Venice and having drug problems. I got into a fight and was cut badly on the hand. Needing help in a hurry, I went to Aunt Jo, who was thrilled to see me and mended my wound. Later, I realized it never occurred to me to turn to Mom.

The depth of Mom's rage at Jo, and her dedication to keeping her out of our lives, was made clear to me in 1986. Mom and I went out to dinner at a Chinese restaurant in Los Angeles. Over appetizers Mom said casually, "Oh, did you know that Aunt Jo died? It was about two years ago," and revealed that her death had been from an excruciating form of cancer.

I was stunned to receive the news in such a way, and I was so upset that I had to leave the table. How, I wondered, could she seem so offhand about it? Not until I discussed the issue with Jodie did I understand more. After I poured my heart out about how flattened I'd been after hearing the news, I expected her to sympathize. After all, her first word had been *Jo*, not *Mama*. Instead Jodie shrugged and said, "I never knew her that well."

I was astounded at first, thinking of all the time we had spent in Jo's care. I wanted to bring out a stack of photos I had of Mom and Jo and all five kids together. But then I thought of Dad. Like him, Jo had become a source of friction in Mom's life, and I couldn't help wondering if Jodie's seeming indifference toward Jo's death wasn't a reflection of her tremendous loyalty to Mom and her antipathy toward anyone who threatened Mom's happiness.

Ironically, considering their tempestuous first meetings, Jo and our father had become friends after she and Mom broke up. They ran into each other by pure accident, and because they were both very genteel, mannerly people, they stopped and exchanged greetings. After a chat in which Jo told Dad of the split, he invited her to lunch. Of course, they had a lot in common: years spent with Mom. The curious relationship lasted until just before her death.

Today Dad regrets very much that he reacted hostilely to her in the first place. "In those days a lesbian relationship was just incomprehensible. If I had it to do over again, I certainly would have been far more understanding. Jo was a wonderful lady. I'm so glad I got the chance to find that out."

In the last months of her life, Jo had begun writing her memoirs and had recorded many tapes, talking about all aspects of her life. But just before dying, she deliberately erased every one of them. I can only imagine she feared she would have hurt those close to her, particularly Mom. It was a compassionate gesture and an ironic reminder of the kindness and humanity she brought to our lives. They were qualities we would all miss over the next few years.

In 1971, although *Mayberry* was still rated in the top twenty of all TV programs, CBS announced we were being cancelled. The official explanation was that the network wanted to cut back on its "rural-oriented, family programs." As the country bumpkins were shown out the back door, *All in the Family* and company were welcomed in. CBS buried the idyllic, country-life fantasy and ushered in the era of gritty, in-your-face, urban hyperreality. It was quite a jarring transition from Andy Griffith and Aunt Bee to Archie Bunker and Meathead.

I was naturally crushed by the cancellation, but Mom was upbeat, trying to be supportive and comforting. She assured me my name and work were known and respected. I would have all the TV work I wanted and would be able to break into movies, just as Jodie had.

For now the balance had shifted. Jodie's career was well underway. Even by the time we moved into Cahuenga Terrace, Mom's focus was shifting from my career to Jodie's. *The Courtship of Eddie's Father* had led to regular guest spots on *Gunsmoke*, the most highly rated show in that era. But Mom had bigger plans. She sensed that concentrating on making me a TV actor had been a mistake. Once a child actor, or any actor, becomes a TV regular, making the transition to movies is almost impossible. Seeing my career hitting a dead end, she decided Jodie would instead be a movie star.

By 1970, when Jodie was eight, she was auditioning almost exclusively for feature films. In 1971 she landed roles in two. The first was a frothy Disney flick called *Napoleon and Samantha*, which was Michael Douglas's first starring vehicle. The movie, shot in Medford, Oregon, had an unlikely plot in which two kids adopt a retired circus lion and turn it into a cuddly pet. Jodie and Mom quickly learned that filmmaking is vastly more realistic, complex— and dangerous—than TV or ad work.

Numerous scenes required Jodie to interact with a full-grown lion that was very capable of killing her. The handler assured Mom that the beast would be so drugged it wouldn't attack Jodie. Unfortunately, things didn't go exactly as planned. Before a particularly tricky scene was to be shot, a substitute lion had to be used at the last minute. The stand-in lion had been kept in a cage parked in the open all night. Neighborhood kids had apparently been taunting the beast all morning and had even fired BB's at it.

As soon as the opportunity presented itself, the enraged animal grabbed little Jodie in its jaws and shook her as a cat does a mouse. Everyone on the set panicked and ran. The trainer ran up and said to the lion, "Drop it." To Jodie's intense relief, the animal did. But it had bitten her deeply, and she was seriously injured. The next thing she knew she was on a stretcher in a Medivac helicopter, being flown to a hospital in Portland. Jodie's abdomen still bears the puncture marks. When I saw the wounds, on both sides of her body, they looked like shark bites.

It would have been quite reasonable if Jodie had decided to end her movie career then and there. Instead she soldiered on, returning to the set several days later to complete the film. Incredibly, a few weeks later the same lion lunged at her again, but that time she was able to leap out of the way.

Napoleon and Samantha was a hit, and the *New York Times* called Jodie "saucy" and "appealing." Unfortunately, her second feature outing was a bit role in *Kansas City Bomber*, a true bomb. The star was Raquel Welch, who played a tough but good-hearted roller derby queen who befriends Jodie. Critics called it "unintentionally funny." It wasn't a particularly auspicious start, but Mom had succeeded in making Jodie a movie actress. She had gotten a foothold in the movie world, where the multimillion-dollar payoffs are found.

In 1973, Jodie and Mom were gone for what seemed like the whole year, making two more feature films, *Tom Sawyer* and *One Little Indian*. Jodie and I auditioned for *Tom Sawyer* the same day. I was deemed too old for the lead role, but Jodie won the Becky Thatcher part. (As Becky, Jodie taught Tom the meaning of the word *philanderer*, which I found amusing, since it was an epithet Mom had regularly hurled at Dad.) This time Mom's instincts were right on the mark. The *Tom Sawyer* remake was critically and financially a smash.

Jodie's small role in *One Little Indian* was opposite James Garner. Garner was amazed by Jodie's acumen at such a young age. Years later when they worked together for the second time, on *Maverick* in 1994, the veteran actor fondly remembered working with her as a child. "She had a presence even then. She was such a little pro, it was amazing. And she was the nicest guy in the business," he laughed.

Upon her triumphal return from the back-to-back movies, all Mom could talk about was Jodie, a habit that has understandably grown over the years. She also began collecting the memorabilia that became the "Jodie shrine," which now includes sculptures of Jodie, oil paintings, Oscars, plaques, and awards. Needless to say, it was a bit hard for me to take at the time. I certainly was proud of her and wouldn't deny her the full measure of accolades, because she deserved them, but I felt pushed out and couldn't help but feel jealous.

I wasn't alone. As Mom spent more and more of her time on distant movie locations with Jodie, my older sisters and I started to get completely out of hand. The only adult supervision we had was from our maid, Blanca, who was afraid of us and avoided any confrontation, no matter what mischief we were up to.

There was plenty. Perhaps the worst came when Cindy hatched a plan to get some additional spending money to blow on pot, which she was regularly smoking at home and with a group of unsavory friends. A few of these characters offered to burglarize our house and split the loot with her. They promised to ignore Mom's precious antiques and only steal a few cases of French wine and perhaps the stereo. Cindy established an unassailable alibi by being at a party with Connie and me, and when we walked back into the ransacked house, she acted as surprised as we were. (Though she fessed up to Connie and me years later, I don't know if she ever told Mom.) It was an absurd and wicked plot, but it shows how far my oldest sister was drifting without supervision. So was I.

I was fourteen then, and I thought I had already been around. I regularly wore my sharp-looking suede and lambskin jacket, and was proud to feel a part of the Hollywood in-crowd. Hell, Elvis was a fan of mine. A few months before, the first time Cindy invited me to come to a party in Encino with her drugged-out hippie friends, I had jumped at it. When we arrived at the party, though, I recognized I was out of my league. Everybody was seriously messed up: drugs ranging from pot and speed to LSD and other hallucinogens were being used. To my surprise, some of the long-haired stoners were my age or even younger. Of course, when the marijuana was passed around I took some because I didn't want to appear uncool. But in trying to fit in with the zoned-out valley kids, I went a step too far.

Cindy always claimed that I asked for some LSD; my recollection is that somebody slipped it to me. Regardless of whose memory is correct, I went on one hell of a bad trip. As soon as the drug took effect, the world looked like a colorized *Mad* magazine; faces had razor-sharp, snapping fangs, and fire gushed out the backs of people's heads. I was so horrified, I just curled up in the fetal position and sobbed. Finally, Cindy led me outside to a van and told me to sit on the hump. The battered old Ford Econoline bumped and vibrated down Ventura Boulevard at twice the legal speed limit, as five or six hippies in the back smoked pot, blasted rock music, and laughed maniacally. I could do nothing but suffer in silence and pray the drug would soon wear off.

After a wild ride through the valley, we stopped at a Denny's for coffee. The fluorescent lights and orange plastic seats of Denny's were exactly what I didn't need, so I crawled under the table and held my knees to my chest. Cindy wasn't concerned with me in the least. I could have stayed under the table all night as far as she was concerned. Fortunately, Connie heard from one of her friends what was going on and came to rescue me. Appalled at what had happened to her little brother, she showed me to yet another car—where the music was along the more soothing lines of "Nights in White Satin"—and took me home. After the effects of the drug finally wore off, I swore I would never get messed up again. That was a promise that I wish I had kept.

The seeds of rebellion were growing in me. I felt as though I had been a star all my life and began to think that giving it up wouldn't be so bad. I wanted more than any-thing to be like the other kids, to hang around after school, get in fights and just be normal. I loathed the thick the-atrical makeup. Every day that I was working, when I got home I would scrub my face until it was almost raw and bleeding to get rid of the pancake. Too many times kids on the street had seen it and teased me mercilessly for being an "actor pansy."

When young people started wearing their hair long, I wanted to have long hair as well. But instead I had to look like a model child from some imaginary small town in the rural South, with very short hair. *Mayberry* producer Bob Ross had told me: "In Mayberry boys don't wear their hair long. Cut your hair. Period." The prospect of being a nobody again didn't seem so bad. In fact, I was determined to see a number of things changed.

One of my worst problems was growing up in an all-female household. "Boys versus girls" had been a frequent battle theme in Granada Hills, when Chris and I had been two against five. In the Cahuenga Terrace house, where I was the only male, the pressure was worse. When I started to display an adolescent's typical anger and frustration, I was sure my mother and sisters all turned on me at once. Stomping my feet and cursing my lot in life made my sisters fear I was growing into something they had always feared and hated—our father.

Even Jodie was very disappointed in me. She was going along with the program, while I seemed to be moaning and complaining about everything. She thought our show busi-ness lives were wonderful and felt there was something seri-ously wrong with me because I no longer agreed. The idea of my abandoning the bonds we had shared as child actors irritated and confused her. The look in her eyes said I was a traitor, and she underscored that after each of my run-ins with Mom by saying, "Look what you're doing to Mom."

At the time I felt Mom, Jodie, Connie, and Cindy just weren't being sensitive to the emotional needs of a boy. In my mind, Mom's mantra of how unfaithful and unreliable men were started to seem to be aimed at me. My father and I were the ones to blame if Mom was unhappy for any reason. It seemed logical that my career was being rapidly eclipsed by Jodie's because she was of the favored gender. I thought that if I had been a girl I would have still been the star. Any attempt to get along with my family or try to reinvigorate my career struck me as futile.

Despite my sullen attitude, Mom tried very hard to save me and my career, an effort I failed to appreciate at the time. She finally came to understand that I needed a male role model, so she went to a group called Big Brother, which paired young men in need of guidance with volunteers. They sent me Joseph Devonee, an insurance executive who really cared about young people. He tried to save me, from myself as well as from my sisters and Mom, who at the time I felt were trying intentionally to drive me completely mad. For a long time, since those miserable Saturday afternoons waiting for Dad, my dream had been for a father figure to take me to sports events and the other boy things I had missed out on. Antique shows and art galleries were fine as far as they went, but I wanted something different.

The days spent with him were wonderful and made me feel like a regular kid, from a regular family. We played with his big standard poodle show dogs, I helped with yard work, and we talked about sports. His wife, a Max Factor cosmetics executive, was a wonderful woman who treated me like a son. For a year and a half he devoted a great deal of time to me. We went to all the U.C.L.A. football and basketball games, and even on a skiing trip to Park City, Utah. But eventually I stopped seeing him, mainly because I was a bonehead who wanted to hang around with a crowd that would bring me only sorrow. But he was truly a wonderful guy and he tried. He couldn't save me at that point, but his influence was a positive thing that I carry to this day, and for that I will be eternally grateful.

Mom valiantly continued to try to steer me in the right direction. She thought if I could stick with show business that I would regain the sense of purpose and discipline I had in the beginning of my career. She and Toni made an effort to get me into feature films, and in 1972 Mom and I went to Valdosta, Georgia, where I filmed *Sixteen* with Mercedes McCambridge. *Sixteen* was followed by *Black Noon*, which starred Ray Milland. And I kept busy with TV, guesting on *Adam 12*, *Dragnet*, *The Rockford Files*, and *Emergency*. But my heart was no longer in it. I had also started to smoke marijuana regularly, which further sapped my concentration and focus. Consciously or not, I had made up my mind to quit show business.

In the meantime, Jodie was on a roll. True, there were other young women in those years who were as well known as Jodie, such as Tatum O'Neal, who won an Oscar in 1974 for *Paper Moon*. But alone among the child actors of her generation, Jodie was able to make the transition to full-fledged adult star.

That achievement depended on her ability to tap tremendous reservoirs of talent, emotional resiliency, and determination. In fact, Jodie eschewed the label "child actor." She told one interviewer, "Being a child actor means being a small actor, and I was never a small actor; I was simply an actor." That deliberate swagger and almost brazen self-confidence was, and is, the engine behind the Jodie Foster phenomenon.

If self-confidence was the engine of Jodie's career, the frequent mechanic under the hood was Mom. Jodie's bond to Mom remained very strong and grew even stronger. They were inseparable, and whenever Mom laid out a new challenge, Jodie embraced it and mastered it. But she was also beginning to establish an identity that was more than being the daughter who could please Mom in everything. In defining herself as something more than Brandy Foster's perfect daughter, she chose her battles carefully, picking issues that would become noticeable parts of the carefully honed image that Jodie enjoys today.

SIX

When I was a kid, while other kids were sitting around worrying about zits, I was making movies about real subjects.
　　　　　　　　　　　　　　　　—JODIE FOSTER

Unlike many child actors who are taught by studio tutors and isolated from the real world, Jodie and I, at Mom's insistence, were always full-time students in addition to working. And up through sixth grade Jodie attended public schools in Hollywood.

For six years Jodie went to Cheremoya Avenue Elementary, in the heart of old Hollywood, a stone's throw from Paramount Pictures. For junior high school Jodie was accepted by one of the most prestigious, and highly rated, schools in Los Angeles, the Lycée Français. The lycée was a perfect place for a young woman who was growing more famous every day, because the student body counted among its members children of Hollywood's top executives, stars, writers, and directors. Instead of being a freak and a curiosity as she would have been at public school, she fit right in. Other than a little gentle teasing there was no special notice whatever for her budding fame.

Jodie found life at the lycée stricter and more regimented than anything she had ever experienced. Girls wore starched white shirts and dark blue uniforms; boys dressed in dark blue pants, white shirts, and ties. Students were required to snap to attention when teachers entered the room, and the homework assignments were demanding. Jodie ate it up.

She had always been willing to go along with any program that promised her what she wanted, and the lycée's academic program outpaced anything public school offered. By this point her knowledge and skills were also far beyond the point where Cindy, Connie, I, or even Mom, could really teach her or show her anything new.

Instead of socializing, her free time was devoted to homework and extracurricular reading. She would retreat to her room and enter a private world populated by the characters of J. D. Salinger novels and *Madame Bovary*. Even Mom knew not to interfere with this time.

When Jodie wasn't working or cooped up with a book, she would often spend weekends when Mom was away with the Kabbaz family, who owned the lycée. They provided structure and watched over her, and the closeness one might expect in a substitute family developed. The Kabbazes' daughter, Clara Lisa, was one of Jodie's classmates, and they have been friends ever since.

Kabbaz recalls, "Nobody treated Jodie like a star. She was just this tiny blond head, with big glasses on, who sat in the back of the room reading."

Still, even if Jodie didn't lord her status over her school-

Our father, Lucius Fisher Foster III, approximately one year before he met our mother. He retired as a full colonel in the air force.
Courtesy of Lucius F. Foster III.

Mom dressed to kill in the fur stole and diamond ring that Dad gave her—and which she later pawned to care for us. *Courtesy of Buddy Foster.*

Our third parent, Josephine Dominguez, in her early twenties. We called her Aunt Jo or Jo D. and were so attached to her that our baby sister was called Jodie in her honor. *Courtesy of Chris Hill.*

This is the house our mother was raised in and where she watched from the window as her father was secretly having an affair with a neighbor. *Courtesy of Rochelle Law Wagener.*

Family photo, 1961, with me, Mom, Cindy, and Connie. *Courtesy of Buddy Foster.*

Chris and me doing our fashion show designed by my sister Connie, 1962. As you can tell, we are not pleased with showing so much leg. *Courtesy of Chris Hill.*

Mom recovering from Jodie's traumatic birth. *Courtesy of Chris Hill.*

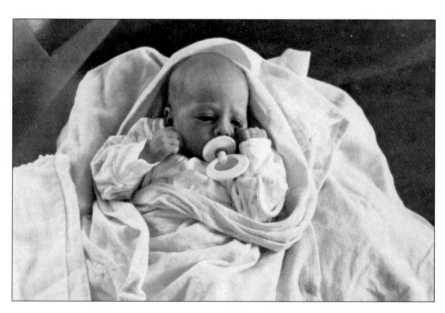

Jodie just home from the hospital in November 1962 with her pacifier, a.k.a. *"Chepon"* in Spanish, thanks to Aunt Jo. Jodie never went anywhere without it until she was four years old. *Courtesy of Chris Hill.*

Our house on Blackburn Drive, where Jodie and I proudly rode our dog, Hondo, around the block. *Courtesy of Rochelle Law Wagener.*

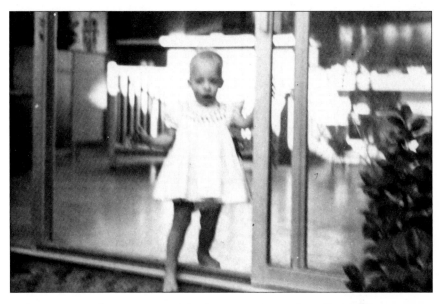

Jodie, 1963, on her way out of the house in Granada Hills to follow us kids. By the time she hit the sidewalk, the sundress was history. *Courtesy of Chris Hill.*

Chris and me dressed as twins, as usual, and I got caught sucking my thumb and picking my nose. *Courtesy of Chris Hill.*

Our beautiful Mom posing for Dad.
Courtesy of Chris Hill.

Chris, Jodie and me in front of the house in Granada Hills, 1963. I can't imagine we stayed in these clothes very long. *Courtesy of Chris Hill.*

Mom during her early courtship with Aunt Jo. *Courtesy of Chris Hill.*

Our mother, Evelyn,
a.k.a. Brandy, looks as
though she has just
seen a man in
uniform!
Courtesy of Chris Hill.

Aunt Jo and Mom during a happy moment together,
1967. *Courtesy of Chris Hill.*

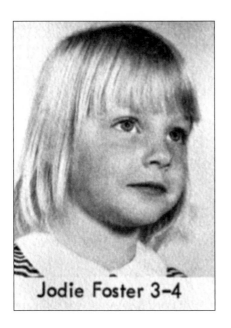

Jodie's first professional
photo for job interviews.
Courtesy of Tori Kelman.

Jodie and Chris in Newport Beach, 1967, just waking up in their
favorite pajamas. As you can tell from the dirt rings around Jodie's
sleeves, you could not get her out of these pj's.
Courtesy of Chris Hill.

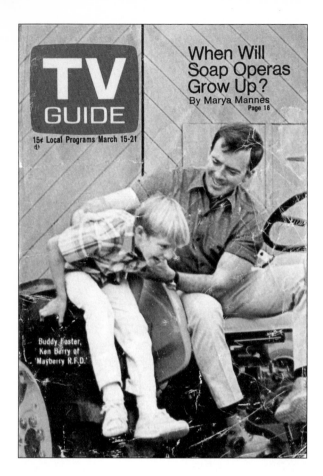

My first *TV Guide* cover, March 1969, with Ken Berry, who played my father on *Mayberry R.F.D.* *Courtesy of* TV Guide.

Jodie with her love dog Napoleon and Aunt Jo doing her Elvis thing, 1973. *Courtesy of Chris Hill.*

Me during the shooting of *Hondo*, 1967. It was my first job as a series
regular. *Courtesy of Warner Bros.*

The cast of *Mayberry, R.F.D.* Our second *TV Guide* cover, July 1970. *Courtesy of TV Guide.*

My first television series role in *Hondo*, which lasted for one season. *Courtesy of Warner Bros.*

This is a continuity
picture taken for
Angel in My Pocket.
Courtesy of Universal Films.

A scene during the filming of *Angel in My Pocket*, a feature movie, in which
I costarred with Andy Griffith. *Courtesy of Universal Films.*

Connie Foster

Connie's first professional photo for job interviews. She was a little too meek to make it.
Courtesy of Toni Kelman.

The Toni Kelman Agency

Aunt Jo, Jodie, Connie, and Cindy taking a trip to the zoo, 1967. I was probably working on *Mayberry, R.F.D.*, so Aunt Jo was the caretaker for the rest of the clan.
Courtesy of Chris Hill.

Aunt Jo snapped this photo of Chris, Connie, Jodie, and Mom on a 1970 trip through the wine country of Northern California. *Courtesy of Chris Hill.*

Jodie during a Crest Toothpaste commercial in 1967. Hey! Isn't that my T-shirt she has on? *Courtesy of Procter & Gamble.*

Jodie with her doll Babar, which she took everywhere. *Courtesy of Yorum Kahana, Shooting Star.*

mates, her life was that of a star's. Since grade school the variations in her schedule were a daily reminder to kids that she was different, as was the limousine that picked her up to take her to the set after class, let alone what they saw on television and movie screens.

If that wasn't enough to isolate her, there was always her adult approach to everything. It made her singleminded in her pursuit of schoolwork. She was always the student who had the assignment done early, always the first to hand in a test, and her drive increased the barriers between her and other kids.

All the same, she wasn't the object of ridicule like Fred in *Little Man Tate*; she could get along. Lycée students remembered a Crest commercial in which Jodie's screen father said, "Be quiet, Jodie," and teased her with the line, Clara Lisa Kabbaz recalls. Jodie and a few of her girlfriends even came charging into class one day with their mouths full of water and spat it in long streams over the heads of the boys in revenge for a year's teasing and ponytail pulling.

Needless to say, Mom was furious when she heard about the water incident. It wasn't the mature behavior she expected. But it was about as wild as she got.

Mom was sure she had made the right move in sending Jodie to the lycée when Jodie became acquainted with Marlon Brando's son Miko, who was later Michael Jackson's super-burly bodyguard. While we were growing up, Mom was fascinated by Brando. There were books about him all over the house, she took Jodie to every movie he ever made, and once she even sat through every showing at a Brando film festival. So having her daughter schoolmates and friends with one of the great man's children was quite a thrill. Jodie wasn't awed in the way Mom was, but she liked Miko. "He was a great kid, a big goofball," she said.

Lycée teachers worked hard to continue challenging Jodie, because if they didn't keep her engaged, she would pursue her own interests and gallop ahead of the class. While most of the other students struggled to master French grammar and pronunciation, Jodie took Italian as well and was soon fluent in both. Thanks to being partially raised by Aunt Jo, she already had a proficiency in Spanish. Of all her considerable educational achievements, she is proudest of her fluency in foreign languages because it gives her the ability to understand other cultures. Jodie developed a lifelong love affair with France and her culture. Her Francophile tendencies thrilled Mom; unlike the rest of us, Jodie was blossoming into the haute-culture child she fervently wished to create.

All her interests, educational and professional, left her little time for goofing off and developing friendships with the other kids. Jodie seemed to be constantly surrounded by people, but always alone. "I have to say—and I didn't realize this when I was younger—I didn't have friends," she later admitted, looking back on her lost childhood. "I didn't start playing until I was seventeen."

Jodie's scholarship, dedication to her childhood acting career, and incredibly even temperament were all the more remarkable considering her two older sisters and brother were constantly in trouble and without direction.

The heavy doses of positive thinking that Mom and Jodie applied when thinking about her career were often needed. Despite Mom's efforts to concentrate on building Jodie's

reputation as a film actress, she wasn't above pursuing television work, which had the benefit of bringing regular pay-
checks. Just after *Courtship* was cancelled, Jodie won a role
on *My Three Sons*, which was one of television's most
popular and long-lasting shows, running for twelve years on
two networks. Just when it seemed she had a regular job she
could count on, the show was cancelled.

There was another small role on the TV series *Bob and
Carol and Ted and Alice*, which was similarly short-lived. She
did win a small part in a television film, *Smile Jennie, You're
Dead*, in 1974, which was the pilot for David Jansen's successful series *Harry O*, but she didn't make it into the
regular program. It seemed nothing would last.

Then that same year, in a strange twist, Jodie found herself up for a promising TV role based on Tatum O'Neal's
Paper Moon film character. ABC offered $425 per week,
which was the standard pay for a child actor. With four films
on her résumé, Jodie and Mom agreed she deserved more. It
bothered Jodie that she was being tarred with that hateful,
demeaning "child actor" brush. Toni Kelman told ABC that
her price was $1,000 a week, period—an unprecedented
demand at the time for an actress without a high Q rating,
which is an indicator of the public's affection. It was a big
gamble. In the end the network blinked, and Jodie rose to a
higher rung on the Hollywood food chain. At last things
seemed to be falling into place.

Unfortunately, *Paper Moon* was broadcast that fall opposite CBS's powerhouse hit *The Waltons*. Jodie and I were
well coached in the art of accepting rejection gracefully;
failure was another thing. *Paper Moon*'s demise after a single
thirteen-week season was a bitter disappointment for Jodie.

She saw it, in part, as her failure and vowed it wouldn't happen again. While the battle-hardened veterans around her (like Mom and me) thought that she was taking the result of an unlucky airtime far too personally, Jodie felt that part of the fault was hers. Tatum O'Neal had played the role with an aura of a certain softness; Jodie's character of Adie was harder, more adult, something critics noted. Jodie wasn't able to shake her sense that she had limited the show's appeal.

She also realized she had made a mistake in following someone else in such a high-profile part—she recognized that she would never be what the public expected. She has never followed anyone else in a role again. It was an unhappy time, yet *Paper Moon* steeled her for other blows to come, both professionally and personally.

Her next opportunity came fast. In the summer of 1974, Toni Kelman managed to get Jodie an audition with one of the hottest young directors in town, Martin Scorsese, who was preparing to direct *Alice Doesn't Live Here Anymore*. *Who's That Knocking at My Door* and *Mean Streets*, Scorsese's dark, autobiographical first films had garnered him a reputation as an innovative director, one of those to whom critics were applying the high-flown term *auteur*. Mom had loved *Mean Streets* and, according to Jodie, dragged her to see it four times.

The opportunity to leap from the forgettable Disney flick *One Little Indian*, her last film, to the small but well-drawn role of the precociously debauched, wine-drinking, shop-lifter Audrey in *Alice Doesn't Live Here Anymore* was too good to pass up. Scorsese remembers well the day Jodie strode purposefully into his office at age twelve to say she had read the *Alice* script and wanted the part.

"Jodie walked into our office on the Burbank lot, and she had total command. A total professional, especially at the age of twelve, is very reassuring. You can rely on their instincts, and their ability to show up on the set and do the work and be ready and willing for anything and be in a good mood about it. That's terrific, and extremely rare."

Mom and Jodie spent much of the summer of 1974 in Arizona, where the filming took place. At the end of the shooting, Scorsese was so pleased with Jodie's performance as Audrey, he made up his mind to offer her an even darker role in his next, and most controversial movie to date, *Taxi Driver*. Portraying thirteen-year-old hooker Iris forever changed Jodie's life, in good ways and bad.

"When Brandy read the script, she was outraged," Toni Kelman recalls. "She said there was no way in hell Jodie was going to do it."

"I argued that it was a great opportunity, but she wasn't having any of it. I said okay, but I didn't call the producers back with a no. I thought I'd wait. Then she called back with a completely different attitude; Jodie wanted the part. I assume Jodie read the script herself and said, 'I'm going to do it.' "

The decision was a first step at seizing control of her career, and it also represented a palpable shift in Jodie's attitude toward acting itself. "I felt so good after seeing myself in *Taxi Driver* that I no longer want to be president of the United States. I want to become a serious actress," she said when the movie was released.

Word of the sensational nature of the role quickly got around in Hollywood and began to stir outrage. State welfare authorities decided a psychological profile would have to be done before Jodie would be permitted to accept the role. The suggestion that adults were trying to exploit her, and that she was a helpless babe in the woods, ruffled Jodie's feathers. Far from being naive and unaware of what she was getting into, she was fully aware of every nuance of the Iris role. Her telling comment at the time was incredibly astute for a thirteen-year-old: "Intellectually, I'm an adult, but emotionally, I'm equal to my years."

The required profile turned into a half-hour inquisition, during which Jodie was asked what kinds of things she did with her friends, what kinds of food she ate, and what movies she went to. Perhaps to the surprise of the psychologist, Jodie announced her favorite films were as adult in content as *Taxi Driver*. They included R-rated *Lenny*, the Academy Award–nominated film about the short, tortured life of fifties comedian Lenny Bruce starring Dustin Hoffman. And *Day for Night*, François Truffaut's movie about making a movie with all the romantic couplings that ensue. The other film she mentioned was also R-rated, *Cinderella Liberty* starring James Caan, a romance about a sailor's affair with a hooker who has an illegitimate half-black son. None on the list were made by Disney.

Edmund Brown, the former governor of California who was then practicing law privately, was hired to steer the way through all the child welfare people's obstacles. (Much was made of this after John Hinckley, Jr., obsessed by *Taxi Driver* and Jodie, shot President Reagan. The fact that Reagan had unseated Brown as governor in a hard-fought campaign and that the two were bitter political enemies was not lost on the press.)

In the end, the skill and clout of Brown, as well as Jodie's ability to remain cheerful—though she deeply resented what she saw as a mindless intrusion into her career—won the day, and she was allowed to take the part.

Having grown up in Hollywood, we were all too familiar with the hookers, pimps, drug dealers, and other denizens of the streets. The Iris character, as Jodie portrayed her, was drawn after the tough yet vulnerable waifs we had encountered over the years in our neighborhood and around our schools.

Still, the child welfare workers watched like hawks during the shooting of the disturbing scene where Iris pushes Robert DeNiro's whacked-out Travis Bickle character to have sex with her. The script called for Iris to yank Bickle's zipper down, which was out of the question as far as the government was concerned. Our older sister Connie had to be recruited to stand in as a body double. Typically, all the demands and compromises were for nothing because the truly provocative bits wound up on the cutting room floor.

DeNiro liked Jodie from the moment they met on the set, and he decided he was going to make her a better actress. During breaks in shooting, he worked with her, going over their scenes until she thought she was going to scream. But the more they worked together, the better the scenes became, and the more Jodie enjoyed acting. The relationship that developed was a lasting one, based on mutual respect; DeNiro became a strong supporter and ally. Jodie even developed an imitation of him that was so uncanny that Scorsese filmed it.

When shooting was finished, Jodie was upset over only one thing: the smell of the fake blood that had been so generously splashed around the set for the slaughter orgy at the end of the film. Otherwise, "it was the most rehearsed, most crafted, most honed performance," she said. "That's what made the satisfaction even greater, to see that if I worked really hard, you don't see the seams."

Taxi Driver turned out to be pivotal to Jodie's career, and Iris a role she is very proud of fighting for. The resulting Best Supporting Actress nomination sent us over the moon, but at the time Jodie was unimpressed. "An Oscar is great, but it won't get me to the beach on Sunday. I'd rather have a car," she flippantly told a reporter.

But years later, looking back on the film, Jodie had a better perspective on what was clearly a breakthrough movie. "That film completely changed my life," she said. "It was the first time anyone asked me to create a character that wasn't myself. It was the first time I realized that acting wasn't this hobby you just sort of did but was actually some kind of craft."

Unfortunately, the film also had a tremendous effect on the mind of a dangerously disturbed young man in Denver. John Hinckley, Jr., began watching the movie over and over, obsessed with both Travis Bickle and the young woman who played the girl he tries to rescue.

At the time, though, Jodie experienced a tragedy that, though more mundane, had a lasting impact on her. She had a little Yorkshire terrier named Napoleon, not after Bonaparte but the character played by young, red-headed actor Johnny Whitaker in her first film, *Napoleon and Samantha*. The dog was a tiny little thing, weighing four or five pounds, with a long, straight, reddish, silky coat that reached the ground. It looked like a little walking wig.

Jodie adored Napoleon. She slept with him, carried him to the sets of her movies, and hated to be separated from the dog. One day when everyone was hurrying around the house to get to work, somebody either stepped on the little dog or kicked him. However it happened, Napoleon cracked his head, went into convulsions, and started throwing up blood. Jodie was panic stricken, virtually in a state of shock, crying and screaming as the animal violently died in her arms. For a teenager without any friends, it was a terrible loss.

Afterward, Mom offered to go out and get another dog. The idea horrified Jodie. She was implacable on the subject: Napoleon had been her dog, he was dead, and she would have no more dogs, ever. Just how deeply she was affected by his death was brought home to me in the spring of 1996 when Jodie finally got the "big slobbering dog" she had wanted for years but couldn't quite bring herself to go out and buy. It was a so-ugly-it's-cute English boxer, with which she has clearly fallen in love. In fact, the dog accompanies her to work, to interviews, and even to movie sets.

I smiled when I realized that after more than twenty years she was at last able to dote on a pet again.

Unfortunately, her hard-won business success came at a time when our family was disintegrating. As Jodie's career soared, I became more certain than ever that I wanted not only out of show business, but also out of my family for good. When I finally broke away, Jodie saw it as a betrayal. Although she has come to understand why I felt I had to leave home, she has never completely forgiven me.

At fifteen, I could no longer stand my mother. There were times when she was wonderful and loving, because she did, in fact, love us desperately. She could be splendidly nurturing and gentle. But I couldn't take the constant flare-ups anymore. The stress of anticipating the next tirade had me constantly grinding my teeth. If I had brought a girlfriend, or just a pal to the house, Mom would shout, "Who's that goddamn tramp?" or "Don't you bring that trash into this house."

Not long after I returned with Mom from Georgia in 1972, we had a huge fight in which I broke nearly half the windows in the house and fled, never to return again. I stayed with Aunt Jo for a time but eventually settled into a rundown apartment, on Bay Street in Santa Monica, which I shared with two older boys. It was walking distance from the beach.

Free from the control of the studios and my mother, I was able for the first time in my life to let my hair grow long and dress exactly the way I wanted to. There were no more wake-up calls before dawn and no more dragging myself home too tired to do anything but crawl into bed.

An unfortunate by-product of my emancipation (as I saw it) was that I dropped out of school at age fifteen. Not until I was in my early twenties did I finally take an equivalency test and get a high school diploma.

By night I worked at a fish and chips shop; by day I surfed to my heart's content. I felt my prayers had been finally answered; I was free of my mother and sisters, and I was going to settle into the life of a normal California boy. Unfortunately, I would soon be caught in a personal maelstrom that would very nearly end my life. And I learned the truth of the cautionary aphorism "More tears are shed over answered prayers than unanswered ones."

The first time Mom and Jodie happened to be in Santa Monica (or so they said), they decided to pay a surprise visit to my apartment. It was a disaster. The flat was full of long-haired, dirty, stoned-out surfers. It was also a wreck, filled with empty beer cans, unminded piles of dishes, and trash.

I had been smoking what I thought was a concentrated form of marijuana, which was in fact angel dust. Needless to say, my friends and I were totally obliterated; Gumby-like, I hadn't the strength to lift my arm and certainly couldn't talk or think coherently. Drugs and requisite paraphernalia were laying out in plain sight. Not surprisingly, Mom came unglued. This was far from the way she envisioned her son living. She fell apart, sobbing and crying woefully. All that would come out of my mouth was meaningless piffle.

Jodie was paralyzed, the spectacle before her a hideous accident from which she could not avert her eyes. A red film of anger washed over my vision, and I lashed out at them both. I felt like I had been apologizing for myself all my life and wasn't going to do it anymore, despite the depths to which I had sunk. The words suddenly burst forth like vomit: "Get the fuck out of my life! Just leave me alone, both of you!"

As Jodie left, she turned and shot me a look of sympathy. I wouldn't have admitted it at the time, but each day that went by after that awful afternoon, I wished that Mom and Jodie would return and rescue me. Years later, I asked Mom why she hadn't forced me to return home. She said a therapist had advised her the best thing was to leave me alone and let me find my own way home. At the time, though, I was so stoned that even though I remember it was Jodie who came to visit me, it could have been Connie or Cindy.

When I knew more about Mom's early years back in Rockford, Illinois, it occurred to me she didn't want to act like her stepfather, Charles Schmidt, when he consigned her to the nunnery for, shall we say, "changes in attitude."

During the next few years I drifted through various dead-end jobs, sold pot to friends for spending money, and lived in a tool shed near Venice Beach, where gang wars raged up and down the strand. My one accomplishment was to free myself of fame; no one knew or cared anymore which shows I'd been on. I was just another surf bum.

Connie was the one member of the family who felt that drawing me closer, rather than shunning me, would help me solve my problems. When she married for the first time, she asked me to give her away. Flattered at the honor, I vowed to stay reasonably sober. But shortly before the beginning of the rather formal ceremony Mom staged at the Cahuenga house, Cindy handed me a couple of quaaludes, powerful tranquilizers. I couldn't resist. Minutes later, when they kicked in, I was all but useless. It was impossible to walk two steps without stumbling, my speech was slurred, and I was incapable of holding anything, including the wedding ring, without dropping it.

It was a shameful display; Connie's wedding was all but ruined. Cindy was the only one who saw humor in the situation, and she shrieked with laughter. Jodie just shook her head and said to me, "You look like the town drunk or something, Buddy. You are really deteriorating." As bad as it was, nobody seriously suggested that I get help. They seemed to think it was just something I would grow out of.

The one person who did try to help was Aunt Jo. She had me read a pamphlet about drugs, which was the first time I realized that I was killing myself. Thanks to Jo, at least I stopped taking pills and stuck to smoking pot.

When I was eighteen years old, my girlfriend, Diana, who was supposedly taking birth-control pills, announced she was pregnant. The idea of being a father at that age, with no money, home, or career, terrified me. I knew that I would get little or no help from Mom because she despised Diana. The fact that she was Mexican-American had little to do with her disapproval. Mom would never discriminate on the basis of race, color, or religion, but she was strictly nineteenth-century when it came to what she saw as class distinctions.

Even I had to admit that Diana and I were polar opposites in most ways. Culturally and socially, we had nothing in common: a fact that eventually destroyed the marriage. But having spent most of my life futilely wishing I had a father at home, I was loath to even consider denying my child. So Diana and I married.

Mom came to the ceremony and, to her extreme discomfort, so did Dad. The restraint it took for the two of them not to have a good go at each other for old times sake was truly impressive. Even so, I caught her hissing, "That bastard," out of the side of her mouth several times. But before the wedding was over they actually shared a dance. That was the most touching part of the whole day.

Diana's family put on a traditional Mexican wedding ceremony and celebration, which included roasting a pig in a freshly dug pit in the middle of a vacant lot and dancing to a mariachi band. To say Mom was appalled would be a gross understatement. On my wedding day, the overwhelming emotion my mother conveyed to me was shame. Not only had I married beneath myself, I had brought dishonor upon the entire family.

Jodie, on the other hand, tried her best to get along with everyone, save for Dad, who she pretended was invisible. She was the only one in my family who genuinely liked Diana and was always very nice to her, but even Jodie thought we were so far apart, in terms of our upbringing, that we were going to have a very hard time making it together.

Shortly after the wedding I went to my sister Connie, who I knew would help me despite Mom's strident disapproval. Her husband then, Chris Dunn, was part owner of the Beverly Hills Hotel parking concession, and he immediately offered me a job jockeying cars. It was a bit ironic that I was parking cars in the shadow of my grandmother's old mansion, at the hotel where she had held court for years.

During that spring Jodie began work on *Taxi Driver,* which would make her a star. But I was far from bitter or jealous; I had a chance to get my life back in order. The tips and salary were enough to rent a decent house and buy a crib for our son, Lucius, who was born on March 6, 1976.

Little Lucius had a profound effect on my outlook. For the first time in my life, I was forced to seriously appraise what my goals were and where I was going. Having the responsibility of a son was trial by fire, but it made me grow up in a hurry. I took Lucius everywhere with me when he was little, and we bonded in a wonderful way. But I still made mistakes with him. Worst of all, I yelled at him, just as my mother had yelled at me and my sisters. I would get torn up inside when I saw the frightened look on Lucius's face. All too well, I remembered how I had felt. Yet I was sometimes incapable of controlling myself. It was a vicious cycle.

I did have a reason to be angry. When I was of legal age to take charge of the money I had earned in my years as a child actor, I received a devastating shock. Despite having earned over $480,000, according to Screen Actors Guild records, which includes only union work and doesn't count residuals for reruns, I had only about $7,000 left. And the state of California had a lien on my assets for $3,200, the federal government one for over $20,000. My dreams of opening a surfboard shop at the beach were all but crushed. I wasn't simply broke, I was deeply in debt.

Mom's response was that I hadn't really earned any money, and what little I had made went for expenses. It was hard to fathom the idea that a child needs nearly a half million dollars in expense money. The method Mom and her lawyers used to circumvent the California state laws meant to protect child actors was convoluted and, when I finally woke up to what had been done to me, infuriating. The scheme started when Mom bought the house on Cahuenga Terrace during the summer of 1968, shortly after my eleventh birthday. Mom's lawyer submitted a report to the court in charge of my guardianship, requesting the court to authorize the purchase of one fourth of the house on Cahuenga with my earnings, which would be held in trust until my eighteenth birthday. This was granted, and Mom was able to purchase the house for $46,000. But in 1976 when I had just turned eighteen, she asked me to stop by her lawyer's office to sign some papers as a "formality."

The lawyer put his arm around my shoulders in a fatherly fashion and told me they were going to transfer my interests in the Cahuenga house to another property Mom was buying. The lawyer, and my own mother, assured me the transfer was in my best interests and would benefit me down the line. In fact, I was assured the profits would be safely reinvested in my name. Nothing of the sort was ever done. Looking back, I obviously should have carefully read the documents, but I couldn't believe my own mother would be capable of taking me to the cleaners. Years later, I learned the paper I had signed that day was a "quit claim," which meant I was giving up my share in the house, turning it entirely over to Mom. After I was gone, they notarized the document and formally stripped me of any share in the house I had helped buy. (On October 14, 1980, the house was sold for $216,500, a profit of $170,500.) But much more was involved than the house. Earnings and residuals from my work in TV, film, and advertisements totalling over $200,000 went into stocks, bonds, and other investments starting in the late 1960s. Thirty years later, that has to be a truly substantial amount of money.

Finally, in 1989 I filed a massive lawsuit accusing Mom and her lawyers of taking part in a conspiracy to bilk me. It was unfortunate that Jodie had to be named in the suit, prompting press attention at the time. But the complex nature of Mom's business arrangements tied Jodie to everything, even though she had no actual responsibility. In fact, Jodie was also a victim, but her reaction was mildly condescending. She said (some years later at lunch) that I was extremely naive, as usual, to have presumed there would be a penny left after I was eighteen. She acknowledged we had both been screwed, but she claimed not to care, an easy attitude to adopt, I thought, when you've been to Yale and get paid a million dollars to do commercials in Japan.

When I filed suit, Mom was appalled. She told me that if I went ahead, I would drag our dirty laundry out in public and ruin my relationship with my family for good. Jodie admitted she hadn't realized how terribly wronged I had been, but told me in no uncertain terms I had to forget about it. Jodie still insisted that as far as she was concerned, Mom deserved the money for working so hard on our careers. But even she admitted we had both "gotten the shaft" and said, "Mom lived wonderfully off both of us." I agreed Mom had worked hard, but I pointed out that Jodie had money left in her trust fund, while I had nothing but tax debts.

Mom would never have been able to talk me into dropping the suit, because I knew she had engineered the whole thing. But I knew that money was not what I wanted. I wanted a thank-you, and I knew I wasn't going to get that from Mom. I dropped the suit and went back to eating myself up over the rotten deal I had gotten. To be painfully honest, though, if I had gotten hold of that money at age eighteen, I might well have killed myself with drugs.

SEVEN

*I didn't exactly grow up like other people. I
didn't start playing until I was seventeen.*
—JODIE FOSTER

ven before the successful release of *Taxi Driver*, 1976 had
proven to be a busy year for Jodie, one in which she
demonstrated her talent in an array of roles. She had
made a tearjerker called *Echoes of a Summer*, costarring
Richard Harris and Geraldine Fitzgerald, in which she
played a terminally ill twelve-year-old. Then came *Bugsy
Malone*, a whimsical Prohibition-era musical about gangland
rivalry featuring an adolescent cast who play their roles as
though they're adults. Jodie played a moll, and Scott Baio
was Bugsy. Both performances were praised as "outstanding"
by *Variety*. Finally, there was the quirky, critically acclaimed
horror film *The Little Girl Who Lives Down the Lane*.

In *Little Girl*, Jodie played an amoral killer who buries
her victims in the cellar of a rented home that she apparently lives in alone. Though just fourteen years old, she

carried the bulk of the rather complex film herself. Her character is on-screen basically the whole movie. Alexis Smith played a nosy real-estate agent who gets it in the end. Martin Sheen costarred as an in-remission child molester who is on to her game.

Ironically, her professionalism and poise seemed to make everyone lose sight of the fact that, beneath the take-charge veteran's bearing, Jodie was still just a child. The film's Canadian producers, who were hoping she would spice up the flick with some pubescent sexual flash à la *Taxi Driver*, quickly learned to respect Jodie's iron will, as well as the sensitive little girl inside.

"This crazy producer kept saying he wanted to pull my dress lower," Jodie said at the time. "I decided he was nuts. I used to tell him to shut up. He really was an idiot; everyone hated him. Finally one day he said, 'We have to have sex and violence in this movie, or the picture won't sell.' I just walked off the set. It wasn't temperament; it was the straw that broke the camel's back. I just said, 'I'm not going to do that.' I talked to the producer and got emotional and started to cry because, well, I'm young, so I cry. And I walked off."

The producer's demand for a nude scene nearly scuttled the production. But at the last minute Connie played peacemaker and offered to act as a body double for Jodie, which settled the crisis. Connie had been doubling for Jodie for years despite the fact she is eight years older and doesn't look a great deal like her. Like me, Jodie is short, fair, and blond. Connie and Cindy both have darker hair and skin and are taller.

But shot from behind or in low light Connie worked as a double. It was not a job she particularly liked, but as in all things, Connie was always there for Jodie and the rest of us when we needed help, advice, or a way out of a fix.

The film was greeted with generally good reviews, and Jodie earned raves. The *Washington Post* called her "a prodigious movie talent in the making," and *People* magazine gushed, "Arguably the best young actress in Hollywood."

Her fee for a movie had grown to $100,000, which was very high for her age and the time, but her growing reputation as a tough customer almost cost her a major role, one she very much wanted, opposite David Niven and Helen Hayes in the Disney movie *Candleshoe*. Writer/director David Swift was outraged when producers told him Jodie was going to be offered the role of the orphan who pretends to be heir to Hayes's estate.

"Anybody but Jodie Foster," Swift fumed. "She has a coldness to her that you cannot warm up to." Whether he was referring to her acting, her steely-eyed persona, or both wasn't made clear, but Swift obviously intended to go toe to toe with the woman-child who at age fifteen had made eleven films and was already a player in the movie business for her insouciant (and scandalous, in some quarters) sexiness. In the end, she stayed and Swift was ousted from his own movie.

But Jodie was far from being a prima donna. She was always willing to work as hard as she could. During the 1976 filming of *Freaky Friday*, which *Daily Variety* called Disney's version of *Lolita*, Jodie suffered an injury during the water skiing scenes. While shooting in San Diego, producers insisted Jodie quickly learn to water ski, something she had never done. With a high-powered speedboat pulling her through choppy seas, there was a painful and dangerous accident in which she suffered a punctured eardrum.

And then the work stopped. Three years would pass before Jodie took another part, in the film *Carny*. She was at a difficult stage. *Freaky Friday* had been very successful for Disney, but it had been filmed before the release of *Taxi Driver*. Although the public seemed to be able to shift from Jodie Foster the teenage prostitute to Jodie Foster the innocent teenager, the movie business was not. Roles for adolescent girls with the weight and seriousness of *Taxi Driver's* Iris were not common in movies, and none seemed to come Jodie's way. As for fluffy Disney parts, those weren't what Jodie wanted.

Instead she was content to concentrate on school and Mom's perpetual program of self-improvement. One gentrified endeavor Mom dearly wanted all her children to embrace was tennis.

Jodie and I frequently went to Larchmont Village, where Mom's good friend Delores Planting lived, to take lessons from a tennis pro, along with Delores's son Drew. Not surprisingly, Jodie proved to be a natural at tennis; she was well coordinated and very competitive. I remember a tournament the pro organized for his students. Although it took place just a few months after Jodie had started lessons, she won her age group hands down. The intensity of her game was intimidating. Playing against her in a doubles match, I found myself the victim of her competitive drive. Every time I headed for the net, there was Jodie, ready to whip my volleys right back at me at top speed. She was so fierce—and strong—in her returns that many of the balls narrowly missed hitting me. Needless to say, my pair lost the match.

Drew Planting, like Jodie, was a straight arrow who, even as a teenager, was very concerned about college and his future career. He told us he was planning to go to Princeton University, then to law school. Education was already important for Jodie, but Drew started her thinking seriously about Ivy League schools and life beyond the movie business. Our family often spent whole weekends at the Planting house, and Jodie, though quite a bit younger than Drew, became very close to him and was influenced by his sensible, conservative point of view.

Through her schoolwork and active independent reading, Jodie was also becoming a genuine intellectual. Conversant with the works of writers such as Baudelaire, André Malraux, and Jean-Paul Sartre, she could easily hold her own in discussions of the currents of French philosophy. She gained fluency in her already good Spanish, and somehow she managed to find the time to get a belt in Judo, skateboard, and play on a girl's soccer team, where her natural athletic ability made her a star.

As soon as Jodie turned sixteen and was old enough to drive, Mom bought her a black 1978 Volkswagen convertible with an all-black interior and top. It was the greatest present she had ever gotten. Jodie has never been a material girl; great wealth, which she started to accumulate at a very early age, didn't excite her or change her lifestyle. The Volkswagen was the exception.

I didn't like visiting Mom in Hollywood, because most of our visits ended in acrimony. So it was nice when Jodie got her car and was able to visit more often. But I was as protective as ever of her and concerned she would get interested in the drugs that were always around. I was taking a nap one evening when Jodie and Cindy came to visit. When I woke up and walked into the living room, they were sitting with Diana. I knew they were smoking pot because I smelled it, though the evidence had obviously been stashed by the time I came in. I went ballistic. I was acting out of more than the natural defensiveness that a brother has for his little sister. I had a feeling that she was perfect and inviolable, and while I was a long way from cleaning up my act, I couldn't bear the thought that Jodie might be smoking pot. But there was no way to stop her. Drugs were everywhere in those days and weren't even considered socially unacceptable by most people. She was going to be exposed to them all the time, and it was up to her whether she would have a problem with drugs or not. But I know I was right to do everything possible to discourage her. I demanded to know if she had smoked it. She swore she had not and said, "I'm not interested in that stuff." Still, I wasn't entirely convinced. Fortunately, Jodie didn't take offense, instead acknowledging my overzealousness in good spirit, a sign once again of her level head.

During her last year at the lycée, Jodie started dating. Mom said at the time with obvious amusement, "Jodie is developing a weakness for small, dark men," though she was as gimlet-eyed as ever in looking over potential suitors. Jodie learned to be extremely guarded about her love life from Mom. When she got such criticism when she brought a potential boyfriend home, she stopped doing it.

It's been widely reported that Jodie's first serious love had actually come two years before, with a young French soldier she met while on vacation in Tahiti, when she was just fifteen. At a New Year's Eve party they were introduced and fell in love at first sight. Even today, she makes it a point to wear the brand of men's cologne he gave her, called Vetiver. The brief relationship still must pull at Jodie because she writes letters to him at his parents' address, hoping they will be forwarded, and she has searched phone books in France when she is over there trying to find him. Surely to her chagrin he has never returned her letters or made any attempt, that she knows of, to get in touch. She once said with melancholy, "It's been so many years since I knew him, but I can still remember absolutely every way that he smiled."

Jodie is not the kind of person who goes around analyzing herself, and she resents the hell out of it when others do. Yet I can't help but wonder if having such an intense first affair end in heartbreak isn't one of the main reasons she has steered so clear of falling for another man.

In 1980, Jodie graduated with honors from the Lycée Français and delivered the valedictorian speech in French, describing herself as "a little girl in blue who stands before you with tears in my eyes." Maybe the long stretch without work had undermined some of her self-confidence, since it was very unlike Jodie to admit to such an emotional reaction to an auditorium full of peers and their parents. There was another sign, too, that Jodie was contemplating the future with uncharacteristic nervousness. Her academic and extra-curricular pursuits earned her letters of acceptance from the nation's most prestigious universities, including, Yale, Harvard, Princeton, Columbia, Stanford, and Berkeley. Mom was out of town at the time applications were due, and Jodie was a nervous wreck, worried that none of them would accept her. The normal college admissions roller-coaster had been complicated by the fact that during her last year of high school, Jodie was juggling applications, final exams, and S.A.T. tests with the production of the dark and peculiar *Carny*. She played a runaway who joins the carnival and gets involved in a love triangle with two born losers played by Gary Busey and Robbie Robertson. Compared favorably to the heavily atmospheric films of the forties, *Carny* was written and produced by Robertson, a member of the rock group The Band, which had started as a back-up group for Bob Dylan and went on to success on its own.

Coincidentally, I was in the area during filming in Savannah, Georgia, shepherding an argosy trailer containing secret panels filled with pot, which I was planning to drive back to California. Though it had been five years since I had moved out of the house, I still clung to some hope that our family might reconcile our differences. Knowing that Jodie, Connie, and Mom were all in Georgia for the film, I stopped by the set, hoping we could renew our family ties. It seemed like a good idea to ask and offer forgiveness all the way around.

Jodie was under tremendous pressure at the time. In addition to a demanding film role, she was feeling the pressure of the impending college decision and the subsequent move that would mean living on her own—without Mom—for the first time in her life. On top of those concerns was the nagging, though at the time, seemingly minor problem, of a clearly disturbed young man named Hinckley, who continuously sent her threatening love letters.

Mom was forwarding the scrawled notes to the FBI and demanding action be taken, but they kept telling her there was nothing they could do unless he did something violent. And that he was probably harmless.

I probably couldn't have picked a more inauspicious time to seek peace. For a variety of reasons Jodie and I had been drifting apart, but I hoped it might not be too late. So one night in Savannah, I said point blank: "Jodie, can't we try to be a family again?" For some reason that set her off. She snapped at me: "Buddy, just get over it. We are not a family, never have been, and never will be. Our father is never going to be there for us, and wishing won't make it so. Just get the whole idea out of your mind. We're not going to help each other out all the time; that's not the way it's going to work."

I was stunned not just at her words but at the fierceness of her tone as well. Our family's way of coping has always been denial; if you have a problem, ignore it. For the first time it seemed to me Jodie was adopting that attitude, at least toward family matters. True, Connie had adopted the active role of family peacemaker, but Jodie had always been the one among us who seemed above the fray. It was, I see now, another way in which we all expected her to be adult long before her time and simply heaped expectations on her without thinking about whether she might be ready to deal with them. Needless to say, I dropped the matter.

The circus sideshow sets of *Carny* were as eerie and nightmarish in person as they were in the film. Dozens of dwarfs, midgets, fat ladies, super-tall men, and other odd characters, who would unkindly be called circus freaks, made up the large cast of extras. And Connie was a body double for Jodie doing a nude scene, which added to the sur-realistic air as far as I was concerned.

So intimate was director Robert Kaylor's look at the characters, critics later called the film "voyeuristic." It was the ideal backdrop for a heavily armed psycho, who Mom later told me was John Hinckley, playing out his role as phantom of the carnival. Several times during shooting, Hinckley was rousted by security cops hired by the producers and arrested by Savannah police, but no charge lodged against him seemed to stick. I was told that the private guards even knocked him around a bit, but that didn't deter him. He was clearly disturbed. He had been sleeping under the carnival rides, sneaking around the set in the darkness, hoping to get a glimpse of Jodie.

The insane letters kept coming, over fifty during 1980 alone. By the time he shot and wounded President Reagan and his press secretary James Brady in front of the Washington Hilton hotel a little over a year later, Jodie had received hundreds of poems, love notes, threats, and entreaties. Typical was a postcard found in his hotel room after the shooting. The scrawled handwriting said, "One day you and I will occupy the White House and the peasants will drool with envy. Until then please do your best to remain a virgin. You are a virgin, aren't you?"

He told her he intended to marry her and that if she spurned him he would kill someone, possibly her. When Mom told me what was going on, I wanted to kill him. Everyone associated with *Carny*, the producers, actors, and security people, went out of their way to try to protect Jodie. They would even have allowed her out of her contract if she had felt too threatened and distracted to continue. But, just as she had come back after being mauled by a lion, Jodie was determined to stick it out despite Hinckley. Then, too, at the time nobody thought he was a real danger to Jodie or anyone else. The feeling was that he was a harmless, if very annoying, nut. All the same, the effect the constant tension had on Jodie was frightening. She was so tightly wound she jumped at the drop of a pin. To ease the anxiety and to pass the time between takes, she played tennis almost every day.

Connie and I tried our best to keep Jodie's mind off her troubles when she was off the set, but it was nearly impossible because she wouldn't cooperate. We tried to get her to come to a great local dance bar for a few beers, but she always begged off, saying she had to be up too early or had to go over the script.

The only time she seemed to relax was a Sunday morning when we all attended services at a black Pentecostal church. Mom had asked the minister if they would mind our attending and was told we'd be most welcome. So on Sunday morning Jodie, Connie, Mom, and I showed up in our Sunday best. At first we were all a bit nervous, but as soon as the spirited singing, swaying to the gospel rhythm, and exuberantly joyous praying began, we were completely caught up and had the time of our lives. That service is one of the fondest memories I have of a family outing during those years. It really felt like we were family again despite all the negative feelings.

After the service was over, we were invited to join the congregation for a barbecue in the church yard with a seemingly endless supply of homemade Southern specialities, the likes of which none of us had ever eaten before. Happily, Jodie was able to relax completely for the afternoon. None of the parishioners made her feel uncomfortable by treating her like a star or even acknowledging she was somebody special.

Of course, it was back to the real world of movie making and stalkers first thing Monday morning.

The part of runaway teen Donna was not a particularly big one, or very well written, but it called for a lot of improvisation, at which Jodie had little experience. And the more she did, the more she gained confidence she could. Despite the problems, she deserves great credit for fleshing out the role and really making it her own. Critics gave the movie four stars and called Jodie's acting "outstanding."

Naturally, Mom was exasperated at not being able to stop Hinckley's harassment. It was one of the times she felt deep regret we had gotten into show business in the first place.

When the film was finally wrapped, Jodie made a final decision about college. The choice came down to Yale and Harvard, with Yale winning out because it was a reasonable commute to New York and she was planning on continuing to work, at least part of the time.

Going clear across the country to attend Yale was hard for Jodie to do. She would be separated from Mom, who had become her friend and partner, as well as her only parent, for the very first time. She was also leaving the house on Cahuenga Terrace, where she had lived for almost ten years, for the last time. Since Connie, Cindy, and I had all moved out, it was really too much house for just Mom and Jodie.

Mom wanted to sell the Cahuenga house as soon as possible and was planning to move to a condo in the valley, where she promised Jodie she would always have a room. But I doubt either of them thought they would ever live together again.

For any young person, going off to college is a sharp transition, but for Jodie, in whose life there were so few permanent, stable things to cling to, the parting was even worse. Constantly traveling to movie sites all over the world and living out of a suitcase in a hotel room made losing the home she had grown up in that much harder.

Before leaving Hollywood, she had her press agent issue a statement saying she would be unavailable for interviews until further notice. She told the Yale administrators she wanted to be known not as Jodie but as Alicia Foster. And she requested her room number and phone number not be listed in the student directory.

But Jodie had resolved she was going to plan out her four years at Yale the same way she would a film. Nothing would be left to chance; every move would be executed perfectly. She could do nothing about who her six roommates would be in gothic old Welch Hall, which happened to be located next to the campus police, because they would be selected by computer. But she did know they would all be girls because Welch was the only noncoed dorm on campus. Jodie hadn't been concerned about sharing a dorm or even a room with boys, but she did want to be located next to the campus cops.

In making her preparations for Yale, she wasn't for a minute thinking about John Hinckley, Jr. His notes, poems, and letters were now going directly to the FBI, and once she left the Georgia location where he had found her, he simply became one of a host of nuts who sent her bizarre mail. At that time she received numerous letters, and a surprising number were from clearly unbalanced souls. Jodie just knew they were out there and wanted to take sensible precautions.

She was convinced she was going to spend an idyllic four years learning about literature and sharing ideas with people as bright as she. No gray clouds seemed to be on the horizon. But before packing for New Haven, she had an obligation to make one more film, the last movie my sister and I would work on together.

Wanting to get back into acting and away from drugs, I had auditioned for a leading role in an independent film called *Foxes*. The movie particularly interested me because the story was written by Gerald Ayres, the father of a friend of mine, and was based on the trials and tribulations of my circle of friends' younger sisters. The film focuses on the lives of four teenagers struggling to come of age in Los Angeles in the late seventies. Drugs, sex, violence, and all the wondrous terrors of growing up whipsaw their lives. At heart, *Foxes* is a bittersweet tale of the close, enduring bonds that develop between a group of teenage girls. One of the central characters is a stoned-out former hooker, played by real-life punk rocker Cherie Currie. That role was based on a girl I dated. In the film she winds up dead from an auto accident just as her life seems to be coming together, though the true story was much happier, though less dramatic. In fact, she checked into a rehab center and got sober. Today she is happily married with children.

The role I wanted was a naive, blond street kid who skateboards through the city and tries vainly to win the hearts and hands of the girls. After auditioning for the part I was given a preliminary nod, but the next day Jodie had a meeting with director Adrian Lyne, who had just signed on. Lyne encouraged her to take the role of the brainy, levelheaded girl in the group. Without knowing that I was up for the part of the kid who woos that character, Jodie agreed.

When Lyne and the producers realized I would be coming on sexually to my own sister, they naturally said I would have to play another part. In addition to actually being brother and sister, we looked it beyond any doubt. Jodie certainly didn't do it deliberately, and I don't blame her at all, but it was disappointing. The part went to Scott Baio.

I tried out for the role of a bad guy who menaces Scott Baio's character, but everybody agreed I wasn't menacing enough. Finally a small part as a drug-addled surfer who picks up one of the girls was given to me as consolation prize.

As minor as my appearance in the film was, I enjoyed it because I had the chance to work with Jodie for the first time in years and for the first time since she had become a star. She had made thirteen movies by that time and certainly knew her way around a movie set; still, I was amazed at how professional she had become. It wasn't simply her skill in front of the camera, but the manner in which she interacted with everyone.

Being a star is a delicate and difficult role in real life. Some people you meet are in awe, some are resentful, others just stare rudely, as if at a freak in a circus sideshow. But almost all of them are looking for flaws, as if to allow themselves to say, "That could be me."

On the set of *Foxes*, Jodie never whined, never made excuses, and never asked people to fetch things for her. She got her own food from the mess line rather than insisting it be brought to her trailer. And she made a point of getting to know everyone. While some top actors give orders that none of the "little people" are to speak unless spoken to, Jodie called everyone from the grips to the truck drivers and cameramen by their first names and would sit and chat with them over lunch.

Her acting had truly become superb as well. Following one of her emotional scenes with Sally Kellerman, as her psychologically close-to-the-edge mother who rants and raves at her,

Jodie had a long, impassioned monologue. When she was done, the crew broke into applause. Coming from a cynical, veteran Hollywood film crew, that was quite a tribute to both women. It was the first time I had ever seen it happen.

As always, Jodie and Mom went on the road for the publicity wind-up, diligently giving interviews, posing for photo shoots, and making appearances to publicize the film. With two films in the can that year, they had their work cut out for them. Having been interviewed regularly since she was about five, Jodie has long had the knack of controlling the interviewer rather than the other way around. She tries to always keep the discussion focused on the film she is promoting and avoids straying into her personal life. These days her publicists make it clear up front that no Hinckley questions will be answered, though even fifteen years after the ordeal his name often winds up in the lead paragraph in the story they eventually run. The other forbidden topic is her sex life; she refuses to gush about how she's fallen in love with a costar or any of the other publicity ploys the Hollywood hype doctors try to get stars to employ.

But that April, Jodie and Mom gave a long, sometimes rambling interview to Andy Warhol for his magazine *Interview*, which broke many of Jodie's own rules. During a dinner with Warhol and his entourage, Mom announced she had become a Muslim and planned to go on a pilgrimage to Mecca. And she said her main concern was for the human rights of the Palestinians. Jodie admitted she had read a lot of Islamic literature but was still agnostic.

I was floored. The timing was execrable. At the time Islamic fundamentalists were holding the U.S. embassy personnel hostage in Iran, and two weeks after the interview ran, eight American servicemen were killed in a rescue attempt. It was not a great time to announce you were enraptured by Islam. Publicly embracing the Palestinian cause was sure to alienate many people in the generally pro-Israeli movie industry. I had known about Mom's passionate concern for Palestinians for years and of her regular gifts to various relief organizations, but that was the first time, I was aware of, that she had gone public with it. As media savvy as Mom had become, I was surprised she had linked Jodie with any truly controversial, divisive political issue.

However, any of Brandy Foster's children can tell you that in her day Mom has expressed enough political opinions, with sufficient passion and force, to satisfy us all. When the marches of the late sixties and early seventies became less common and the Foster party packed up its banners and megaphones, Mom found herself with a small but captive audience. It didn't even really matter if we agreed with her. The oratory flowed. I once made the mistake of saying that while I had no plans to join the military, I would serve if drafted. I felt it was an obligation that I should not duck. (Of course, by the time I was old enough, the draft had ended.) Mom's reaction was the flip side to what Archie Bunker might have said if Edith had burned her bra.

Not surprisingly, Jodie has, over the years, assiduously avoided making any kind of political statement. She has said repeatedly: "I'm not political. It's not part of who I am." Jodie refuses to allow any advocacy groups to make her appear to be a spokesman for them, even if she basically agrees with their philosophy. She instinctually avoids this because the potential for being used is so great. When the time comes to choose a worthy cause to benefit from her premiere parties, Jodie is equally cautious, making sure the organization doesn't have an obvious political ax to grind. The 1995 premiere for *Home for the Holidays* raised money for The Big Sisters Guild, which helps young girls in need. *Little Man Tate*'s opening party honored gifted children. She also embraces AIDS charities.

Anorexia is another special concern because teenage girls were dying of the ailment. In 1980, she signed to do her first TV role since *Paper Moon* was cancelled in 1975, a TV movie on the subject of anorexia, called *The Best Little Girl in the World*.

"I really wanted to hate the script, because I didn't want TV," Jodie said at the time. "But it was the best thing I've ever read. The whole idea of doing the show is to save a life. Everyone knows someone who's had it."

Unfortunately, she was never able to make her dream TV movie because it was delayed by a Screen Actors Guild strike, and by the time it was back on schedule, she was at Yale. The film was made instead with Jennifer Jason Leigh. The loss of the opportunity was a disappointment, but one that was soon forgotten in the fateful year to come.

EIGHT

*Other actors . . . were always so common,
waiting tables or whatever until they were
twenty-five. Now they get to be uncommon.
I like to think my life is in reverse. I was
always uncommon. I'd like to be common.*
                                        —JODIE FOSTER

hen Jodie departed for Yale in the late summer of 1980,
she was like many other young people who leave home
for their first taste of independence. The uncertainty of
leaving Mom behind was mixed with the thrill of not having
to answer to her on the thousand daily points of behavior that
our mother policed. Jodie was also leaving behind, for a time
at least, the rigorous schedule that came with film work.

These changes meant tremendous freedom, but what she was
truly looking forward to was a new challenge, a rigorous course of
academic study. Always eager to learn, the girl who had taught
herself to read by three knew that Yale offered a tremendous
opportunity, and she was going to make the most of it.

Yet Jodie was wholly unprepared on two other fronts. The
drama that surrounded John Hinckley, Jr., was a nightmare no

one could have predicted. Despite all the crazy letters he had sent, she never imagined he would leap out of the darkness and actually become a part of her life. The other shock, however, was an inevitable result of the nature of her life to that point.

Jodie simply didn't know how to lead an everyday life or deal with everyday people. She had to struggle to relate to a new group of peers, many of them equally as gifted and just as self-confident, and almost all of them from normal backgrounds. This was confounding for her. She had always been the wisest one, the most self-possessed, the child who could demand adult treatment. Mom had encouraged this perception by showing Jodie off in front of her friends. Cindy, Connie, and I had reinforced it by the awe with which we treated her. Also, the esteem Jodie had been shown by the likes of DeNiro and Scorsese had furthered the idea. Jodie was used to being exceptional and was accustomed to the deference and automatic respect that it brought. It wasn't that Jodie was arrogant on these points, but she had simply never had to work to fit in before. (Not fitting in in our drama-prone family had actually been a survival skill.)

Because Hinckley reappeared so quickly in the process by which Jodie was learning to make and keep friends, the impact he had was magnified enormously. Without the familiar support of Mom, she was completely disoriented for a sustained period of time, another new experience that was harrowing for her. She was famous for her ability to get a scene right on the first take, and now she couldn't find her mark.

The early 1980s were a crucible in which Jodie Foster the adult was formed. She began to create relationships of choice rather than of family ties, necessity, or professional admiration. And she started gaining an insight into both the depravity and the strengths of which human beings are capable, an insight that was necessary for the powerful work she would create as she came into her own.

Jodie moved into Welch Hall, bringing along a portable Olympic electric typewriter and other necessities of college life. She carried her books around campus tied together with a rubber strap. She was going to do her best to be a normal Yale student.

More than anything, Jodie wanted to fit in and be liked by other students. But the physical trappings were not enough, and she wasn't even sure she'd gotten that part right. She said she felt like a "social retard" because she had never had a childhood and hadn't learned the rules of getting along with young people, didn't speak their language, and didn't dress right. "My whole time at Yale was about wanting to be like everybody else," she lamented a few years later. For her childhood and teen years, Jodie had been in the company of adults almost every moment she wasn't in a classroom, and there she had been focused on the books and the blackboard. The few kids she had known were actors like her and had been similarly socially isolated.

Midway through *Little Man Tate*, six-year-old Fred excitedly enrolls in college classes, only to find himself bewildered and sometimes gawked and laughed at by his classmates. Jodie didn't write that scene, but I know it had a deep resonance for her.

Unused to being baffled by a challenge, she fell back on skills she had mastered a long time ago. "I grew up in an arena where you want to please everybody and you're not supposed to be honest with people," she said. "When I got to Yale, I wanted to be liked, so I lied. If they wanted to hear something, I'd tell them what they wanted to hear." It had worked as an actress and it had worked at home. But it wasn't satisfying, and she was about to learn how shallow friendships based on such shifting ground were.

Not long after Jodie began settling in, John Hinckley, Jr., turned up again. He found out Jodie's dorm and room number and rang her on the phone. Chilling tape recordings of the pathetic, hectoring attempts to court her were later found in Hinckley's boardinghouse room in Washington.

"This is the person that's been leaving notes in your mailbox for two days," he told her by way of introduction when she answered her phone. During one of the conversations there was the sound of girls giggling in the background. Jodie taunted him: "They're laughing at you." Later she tried to scare him off, saying she was waiting for him with a knife. "I'm not dangerous, I promise you," he said. In another conversation she grew angry: "Seriously, this isn't fair. Do me a favor and don't call back."

"How about tomorrow?" he pleaded.

"Oh, God. Oh, seriously. This is really starting to bother me. Do you mind if I hang up?"

"Jodie, please!"

When she stopped taking his calls, he grew desperate and angry. "The most important thing in my life is Jodie Foster's love and admiration," Hinckley wrote in a letter to a *Time* magazine correspondent, discovered after the shooting. "If I can't have them, neither can anybody else. We are like . . . Romeo and Juliet. It drives me crazy just looking at some of her photographs. I tried to rescue her once, and I may have to do it again. I can't take much more of this silent treatment. The ultimate expression of my love would be to take her away from Yale and the world permanently. Further elaboration is not necessary. Just stay tuned."

Hinckley aside, Jodie had classes and a life to get on with and she plunged in. Although she had talked about leaving acting behind, Jodie was soon playing second lead in a Yale production of *Getting Out,* a drama that had been an off-Broadway hit the year before. Perhaps she was searching for familiar experiences to stabilize her new life. Also, because she had never acted on stage before, there was the lure of a challenge that she felt more equipped to master. The role was an emotional one ("I got to scream a lot," she said), with an eerie similarity to the one that had started Hinckley's obsession. She was playing an ex-hooker.

On March 31, 1981, outside the Washington Hilton, Hinckley's dark and demented life reached its nadir as he attempted to assassinate President Ronald Reagan and succeeded in crippling press secretary James Brady. When word swept across the Yale campus that President Reagan had been shot by a man named John Hinckley, Jodie was immediately shell-shocked.

When the initial sense of horror and disbelief wore off, though, an eerie sense of calm and normality set in. At least the psycho was finally behind bars, and would certainly remain there for the rest of his life. Because Jodie had been largely sheltered from his bizarre correspondence, the degree to which Hinckley's obsession with her was tied to his motivation for shooting Reagan was not yet clear to her. Her overwhelming impression was that the madman had been caught and she was safe at last. Incredibly, just at this moment another psycho sprang up to haunt her.

During one of the final performances of the play, Edward Michael Richardson, a twenty-two-year-old mentally disturbed drifter, arrived in New Haven and began to wander around the Yale campus in search of Jodie. Like Hinckley, he had sent her numerous letters, none of which she had read, assuming they were from her primary tormentor. Richardson tracked her down as easily as Hinckley had, and he slipped another letter under her dorm room door. When Jodie read it she was horrified. Instead of the usual confused, rambling mash notes she had been getting from Hinckley, this was a flat-out death threat.

The small circle of friends she had been forming felt she should take the threat seriously and not expose herself by performing in the play anymore. But Jodie was Brandy Foster's daughter. Capitulating would mean sacrificing her freedom, and she wasn't going to do that. Plus, the idea that he would attack her in a crowded theater seemed absurd.

Skulking aimlessly around the Yale campus, Richardson saw a notice advertising *Getting Out*, costarring Jodie Foster, and he immediately bought a ticket. He was determined to finish Hinckley's work. Scanning the audience and nervously anticipating the moment she would take the stage and walk into his line of fire, the would-be assassin took a seat just several rows from the stage. He planned to stand, profess his love, shoot Jodie dead, then take his own life.

But the plan went wrong. When he saw Jodie in person for the first time, he lost his nerve. Richardson later told police he thought she was "too beautiful to die." Sweating profusely and trembling, he stumbled out of his seat, shoved his way out of the theater, and took a bus back to New York.

Furious with himself for not having killed her, Richardson

phoned Jodie's dorm at Yale and claimed he had planted a bomb, which he would detonate via remote control if his hero John Hinckley, Jr., wasn't immediately released from government custody. In the middle of the night, Jodie and her fellow students were forced to evacuate the dorm. Almost as if to ensure he would be caught, Richardson then called the White House and threatened the wounded president. Hours later, Secret Service agents arrested the armed, unbalanced young man at the New York Port Authority bus terminal, and he promptly confessed to all his deeds.

There was no doubt, as one mad event followed another, that her life at Yale was never going to be normal, and whatever fantasy she had entertained of being "just another Yalie" was shattered. Jodie quickly moved from the dorm suite to a more secure single room (dubbed a psycho room—meaning a place where she would be safe from psychos) and got an unlisted phone number. She wasn't like everybody else, not by a long shot. An attempted presidential assassination had lifted her out of the ordinary in a way that would take years for people to forget. And although she obviously bore no responsibility, she felt partly to blame. After all, Hinckley had been set off by a movie she had made at the age of thirteen, and he had shot the president because she wouldn't talk to him. She had inadvertently conjured up evil.

At first Jodie responded to the crisis with an engaged, take-charge attitude. She called a press conference and expressed her horror at what had happened to the president and his press secretary, and at what had nearly happened to her. The room was jammed full of reporters and photographers. Bulbs flashed until she was nearly blinded, and many questions were nearly taunts. Ending with a vow that she had said her last words on the subject, Jodie asked that the press leave her alone. That heartfelt plea was met with snickers. Silly Jodie. There was too much money to be made in exploiting her pain.

The Hinckley affair, which made Jodie the most famous stalking victim in recent history, created a nexus in the collective consciousness between Jodie, President Reagan, and a psycho. Yet even in the face of the onslaught of publicity, she refused to be labeled as a victim (she hates the mere sound of the word). She decided to handle the crisis herself and refused to take phone calls even from Mom, who was growing increasingly hysterical as she watched the news unfold on television. Mom desperately wanted to be by her daughter's side.

As always, Jodie managed to display strength while chaos reigned around her. She did a truly admirable job of getting through the immediate aftermath of the ordeal with dignity, and discovered strengths she didn't know she had. She never would have chosen such a harrowing experience to serve as the break between being Mom's little girl and being her own person. But that was what happened: she was determined to go it alone.

There were some lasting consequences. Jodie became a different person afterward. She was less trusting, more cynical, and much more cautious. Just walking across campus to a class felt like running a gauntlet. University police surrounded her and signaled her presence as effectively as a foghorn. The press was a constant presence—badgering, snooping, and inventing wild stories without a shred of truth. Accompanying this was constant gawking, as though there suddenly was something freakish about her.

At the time Jodie said, "I'd be sitting in the library, and people would run the gamut of human responses. Some were wonderful, and then there were the five percent that fulfill your worst nightmares of how people react under the circumstances. I knew that these were the faces, the uncomfortable, fascinated eyes, that I would have to meet for the rest of my life. I felt like a pariah. And, of course, victim, victim, victim."

The television images were horrible beyond belief and continued to be replayed over the months as Reagan recovered and Hinckley was put on trial. The film showed Press Secretary James Brady sprawled on the sidewalk with a gaping wound in his forehead, the president's stunned look as one of the gunman's explosive Devastator bullets slammed into his chest, a Secret Service man and a police officer crumbling to the pavement with their wounds. It eerily resembled the television footage we had watched, unbelieving, thirteen years earlier when Robert Kennedy lay on the floor of the Ambassador Hotel's kitchen. Only this time my own sister was standing just off camera, a shadowy presence behind the scenes.

The episode was so bizarre that her name became a popular buzzword. Poor-taste Jodie Foster jokes became a staple. A punk rock band called itself Jodie Foster's Army. The incident became a defining moment of the eighties, a pop-cultural event. Little thought was given to the sensitive nineteen-year-old at the center of the tempest.

As if she hadn't suffered enough, things soon took another unfortunate turn. When Jodie was fifteen, she and Mom had decided the time had come for her to pose for some sexy, leading-lady–type pictures. The Disney movie *Candleshoe* had just wrapped; next was the sexy *Carny*, which was going to signal a new direction in her career, the first time she was going to wear some truly skimpy costumes in a movie. Mom felt the new pictures should reflect that

Jodie was a mature leading lady. She chose Italian photographer Emilio Lari, a family friend, a highly respected professional, and someone Mom trusted.

Lari, his wife, and Mom were all present for the session, and Jodie was thoroughly comfortable. At first she posed in a rather demure bathing suit, but Lari, who had been told his job was to get some sensual pictures, encouraged Jodie to slip her top to the side and finally to take it off. Mom smiled encouragingly, and Jodie removed her top completely as Lari snapped away. Finally she was completely nude, save for a towel she enticingly used to cover vital areas.

Mom assumed she would have control over the pictures, and only the ones in the best of taste would be used. All went well until, in the wake of Hinckley's trial, outtakes from the shoot somehow got into the hands of a commercial photo agency in Los Angeles, which began to market them. One of the first to get the pictures was *High Society*, a semi-porn magazine that specializes in printing nude or seminude pictures of celebrities. Most of them tend to be grainy long lens shots, clandestinely taken on beaches or even over fences. The Lari pictures were a bonanza for *High Society*, and they played it for all it was worth.

Hinckley, as might be expected, tried his best to get someone to send him a copy of the magazine but was stopped when his keepers intercepted a subscription request. However, the pictures were soon reproduced in tabloids all over the world with screaming headlines like *JODIE FOSTER's SHAME: STEAMY PHOTOS COME BACK TO HAUNT HER.*

All of the pressure began to take its toll. In the months after the shooting, Jodie gained twenty pounds, a fact the tabloids trumpeted. Paparazzi, who regularly staked out Yale for the first time in history, documented the extra pounds as unflatteringly as possible. One reporter bribed guards to let him in Jodie's building; a film crew jimmied the door to grab some footage of her. Jodie recalled, "Being photographed felt like being shot; it still does." One photographer, in an effort to keep her from fleeing, knocked her down, causing her to break her clavicle. His shots made, he then jumped up and down in triumph, yelling, "I got her, I got her."

The experiences taught her a considerable amount about whom she could trust. The "friends" who had told *People* magazine tales of her nocturnal cravings for sweets and who accepted "fees" to help set her up for paparazzi attacks were often the very people whom Jodie had worked so hard to emulate. What, then, was the point of working so hard to be liked if this was the reward?

For the first time in her life she smoked too much and drank too much. She hadn't done either while living with Mom, and had just started both in the way that many kids do when they first move out. Soon she was consuming two packs a day. She wore black all the time and grew preoccupied with death. She said later that Hinckley had repeated over and over "I love you" in his insane letters. I'm sure that hearing those three words will never quite be the same for her.

At least she was spared the agony of testifying at Hinckley's trial, where she could have been grilled by his lawyers and asked humiliating questions designed to make her look guilty of something and deserving of harassment and threats. The court ruled she could simply make a video-taped declaration of what had happened to her, which made sense. After all, Hinckley could clearly be seen shooting the president of the United States and several others on a videotape. There was little doubt about what he had done.

Jodie began to find out more about Hinckley, none of which was comforting. His mother was also nicknamed Jodie, and the woman bore an uncanny resemblance to my sister. When it came out that Hinckley was the son of a wealthy Colorado oilman and had a substantial trust fund in his name, Jodie asked her lawyers if she could sue him for pain and suffering. The answer, sadly, was no, because the trust fund had been cleverly written so none of the money was actually in his name. That was one more source of exasperation and anger for her. She didn't want the money so much as she was searching for a way to fight back, to cast off the mantle of victim.

Finally, realizing that her equilibrium was shot, she took a well-deserved vacation in France in the summer of 1981. There she began to write about what she had endured. "I died when I looked at myself in the mirror, the body that no longer slept, the clothes I no longer cared for, the mismatched socks, the tired expression, the reddened eyes, the languid stare. My prior identity—the actress, the enthusiastic collegiate—no longer existed. I wore the same jeans for weeks and wouldn't comb my hair. I had my nasty bouts with tequila and woke up asking 'Where am I?' I got so upset at times I thought I was having a nervous breakdown."

Yet in writing out her anguish, she began to turn a corner. Once back at Yale she offered a well-crafted, sincere piece entitled "Why Me?" to *Esquire* magazine. The editor snapped it up immediately, offering an underwhelming $800 fee, which was a tiny fraction of what a celebrity magazine or major newspaper would have paid. But *Esquire* agreed to Jodie's strict ground rules: there were no pictures, no cover line, and no publicity campaign. She had found a dignified forum for her own views on victimhood. It was time to move on.

In the days and months following Hinckley's attempt on Reagan's life, I didn't speak to Jodie. I didn't have her new phone number, and I didn't try to get it. Mom has always given me hell for not somehow being there for my sister, a reaction I initially suspected arose out of her own feelings of impotence and frustration about the whole affair. But Mom was right, of course. I should have persisted and gotten through to Jodie, and I will always regret not doing it. The remark Jodie had made during the filming of *Carny* about not wanting to be a family was still ringing in my ears. I thought she meant that she didn't want me around anymore, and I was hurt. My weak reaction, I later realized, was a sign of just how much the relationships in our family needed to be mended. In any case, I couldn't have chosen a worse time for a fit of pique; I should have been more sensitive to my sister's needs instead of giving her cause to remember my silence, though Jodie has always had the grace to not mention it.

In my defense, I did have my own share of woes at the time. Although not on the harrowing scale of Jodie's problems, they combined to make this a very bad period in my life.

I said before that the loss of the lead role in *Foxes* was disappointing. It was. I'd been getting by, providing a no-frills life for my wife and my son, and I saw *Foxes* as a chance to put us in a better position. Even an armchair psychologist could tell you that I was recreating the situation that I had known as a child: use acting to get money to buy happiness. It hadn't really worked the first time, and this time around there was a new monkey wrench in the gears. Our relationship was crumbling.

Diana and I have long since gotten over the anger and disappointment of our divorce. We've raised our kids together, helped each other out; we're friendly. But when our relationship was over, I was a wreck. I was angry, I was despairing, I wanted to fight everybody, I wanted to curl up and cry. I'd done what I was supposed to do and I was still getting—well, call it a raw deal.

There was only one part of my life left where I didn't feel like a chump. I had started motocross racing a while before. I was good at it, daring enough to break out of a pack at the right moments. So, I reasoned, if I hadn't cut it as a son, if I'd been screwed out of an acting career and its financial rewards, the one thing I could still do was race. And I could be even better at it than I had ever been. It was my dream to race professionally, and I was very encouraged after winning as top amateur in the Orange County International and collecting trophies in several other contests.

Then, a few months after the completion of *Foxes*, I spun out of control at very high speed coming down a steep hill and was first on the scene of a terrible pileup. Over twenty bikes crashed into me, one after another. Twisted, burning metal and shattered plastic rained down, causing an acute concussion, breaking my pelvic bones, shattering ribs, and fracturing my spine. Unaccountably, I stumbled away from the hellish scene, walked six or seven feet and passed out.

Jodie was at Yale and Mom was in France, so Connie was the first family member to see me in the hospital, lying motionless, paralyzed from the waist down, tubes running in and out of my body at every juncture. I was completely helpless and in excruciating agony. Unfortunately when Connie came to visit, Diana was already in my room. The two women loathed each other, and both were extremely volatile in an emotional situation. Predictably, Connie was in Diana's face immediately, shouting, "This is all your fault! How dare you let my brother do something crazy and almost get killed!"

My feeble entreaties counted for nothing as the argument quickly escalated to violence. Connie and Diana fell upon each other savagely, scratching, kicking, and pulling hair. They shrieked and howled, falling on my bed, sending jolts of pain through my broken body. Terrified they were going to knock me off the bed, breaking more bones, ripping catheters and intravenous tubes out of various tortured body parts, I screamed desperately for help, pumping the emergency call button with all my strength. It took three nurses to pull Diana and Connie apart, and escort them from the hospital with a stern warning never to return.

While lying on my back in the hospital for nearly two months, I was constantly given shots of various powerful narcotics to ease the pain: Percodan, Demerol, Delaudid, and other morphine-based drugs. They did take away the physical pain, but to my surprise they also took away the psychic torment that had bothered me all my life. They seemed to touch my soul, to warm my heart, and to ease the sense that I had that a fight was about to erupt at any moment. It was really terrifying to find that chemicals, which the nurses gave me every fours hours, could so easily and effectively relieve all the anguish.

When the time came for my discharge, the physician who'd overseen my case was away, and for some reason no one at the hospital realized that complications from my extended use of these powerful drugs would result. They sent me off with a merry wave, and unsuspecting, I started picking up the pieces of my life, a process which lasted twenty-four hours, at which point I had a seizure and had to be rushed to the hospital.

This time I went through the standard medically supervised withdrawal process. I licked the physical addiction just fine. But the emotional and psychological addiction was another matter. I craved the freedom from anxiety that the drugs brought. For the first time since childhood, I wasn't grinding my teeth at night. Since I still had a great deal of physical rehabilitation ahead (I was using a walker for the first two months out of the hospital), I easily convinced my doctor that I needed something for pain. I managed to stretch that performance out over the next two years, and when I couldn't cadge a prescription from him, well, there were other places and other ways a guy with my experience could find chemical solace.

The one person who stood by me during that period was my father, who came to the hospital when I was about to be released and offered me a job. He hired me as an employee, but only as an employee. There was no tearful reunion or thought of dealing constructively with the pain of our past. Nevertheless, I learned skills from him in business and construction that have allowed me to make a good living.

One other upside was that I got the opportunity to ask him questions that had nagged me all my life. One hot day, after we were finished working, my father and I sat in my truck, shirtless, drinking soda, and talking at the construction site. It took a fair amount of nerve, but I said, "Dad, why did you disappear after the divorce? Why did you always leave me sitting on the porch waiting for you, after promising to pick me up?" He said very quietly, "I never knew how to be a dad." I remember breaking into a sweat and actually getting dizzy, it stirred such emotions in me. I wanted to say to him, *"The reason I did a lousy job when I was a father at eighteen was because you were never around to teach me how."* But instead, with sadness and resignation rather than anger, I said, "I understand," and drove away.

In the same vein, Dad once told me about his sister Courtney Elizabeth, who died at the age of seventeen from a streptococcus infection, which today would be little more than a bad sore throat, treatable with penicillin. They were very close in age and grew up together. Yet in his telling of the story I couldn't detect a trace of emotion. He didn't seem to hold back any tears at the memory of a presumably beloved sister, stricken in her youth. But that was his way of coping with the loss. He never wanted anyone to see him cry. How could a family so skilled at hiding their feelings produce a two-time Academy Award–winning actress?

In the meantime, my involvement in hard-core drugs deepened. I started shooting heroin in an effort to find an ever more elusive release from emotional torment. There were plenty of times when the smack made sure I didn't give a damn about anything. Mom dropped by my digs in Venice—by now I was living alone in a trailer on a lot I rented for $50 a month—and was horrified. Mom had worked in the jazz clubs of Chicago; she had to have suspected what I was doing. She wouldn't talk about the heroin and other drugs directly—that would have been an admission of failure on her part as a mother, as well as an accusation that might have opened an irreparable gulf. Still, she was outraged by the squalor of my trailer. "How can you do *this*?" she asked me. "How can you live *this* way?"

So even though she wasn't able to confront me on the issue, it was her voice inside my head that got me back on the right path again. I knew that *this* and *this* way of living were shameful. I was capable of more. I ought to be stronger than this; I ought not to succumb to some outside influence that could leave me passed out in a gutter. It's weird: trying to escape my Mom and the pressures of my childhood were part of what got me hooked on drugs, but it was my Mom's lessons in childhood that helped me get off drugs.

I checked into the Palmer drug-abuse program, which had recently gained a good deal of publicity. One of Carol Burnett's daughters had enrolled and was now clean. The pair of them were working to raise money for the program, which specialized in helping young people with addictions. They certainly weren't the only other high-profile family with kids in the Palmer program, but the only person I'll mention from my time there, because she has talked about it herself, is my friend Eileen Getty.

The Palmer program taught us to completely restructure our lives. Yes, we had to feel whatever pain had led to our addiction. But we also had to get over it, move on, and live life in a new frame of reference that didn't include all the crap that had brought us down in the first place. It was tough, but I liked it. From the basic program in Los Angeles, I went to Houston, then Dallas, and back to Los Angeles. It took two years. I was clean, I was happy with myself, and I didn't define myself by what I could provide for other people.

It was time for me to move on, too.

NINE

A girl I played once has a line that goes "I get up every morning with my dukes up." That's how I'm beginning to feel.
　　　　　　　　　—JODIE FOSTER

Jodie summoned all of her strength to get back on track. She spent endless hours at the gym doing aerobics, yoga, lifting weights, and learning karate and kick boxing, which made her feel more hunter and less prey. She cut out the midnight junk snacks and started cooking her own meals, another page from Mom's book, only she eschewed fancy dishes for a regimen of organic food.

She also developed a small circle of friends with whom she found she did have authentic bonds. Jennifer Beals, who later starred in *Flashdance*, was one of the few people at Yale with whom she could talk show business. Tina Landau, producer Ely Landau's daughter, was another. If being a normal college student was no longer possible, she was able to forge new relationships based on common experience.

Jodie eventually shared a platonic relationship and an

apartment with John Hutman, still a close friend today, who often designs the sets of her movies. For years Hutman was mistaken for Jodie's lover, and nothing they said or their friends said—or even what Hutman's parents, who were hounded on the subject, said—seemed to disabuse the tabloids of their belief.

Hutman tells the story of the day at Yale they cemented their friendship. A super-preppy student came up to him while he and Jodie were playing Frisbee and asked point-blank if it was a fact that he was from Los Angeles. When Hutman admitted it was true, the preppy said, "Then you must be trendy and shallow." From then on Jodie was nick-named "Shallow" and he "Trendy," though the names were interchangeable.

Now, over fifteen years later, Hutman has remained close, and he is almost always involved in her movies. The two have a wonderful, frequently childlike relationship. Typically, while Jodie was deep in the throes of directing *Little Man Tate*, John was able to get her to drop everything, climb on a set bed, and bounce up and down, holding hands, screaming and laughing with glee. Another time, while she was pontificating about her film theories to a reporter, Hutman belched loudly, interrupting Jodie's ardent reasoning and making her laugh. Hutman serves as a constant reality check for her; she needs him around to puncture her balloon when she gets a little too full of herself and to help her let off steam when she gets tightly wound.

"Half the substance of our relationship is me bursting her bubble," laughs Hutman.

Their college apartment was decorated in a style that could charitably be termed eclectic. Hung over a door like mistletoe was a pair of beat-up green Converse high-tops I gave Jodie for a Christmas present. Christmas lights were strung all around. A hundred dolls (which belonged to Hutman, not Jodie, who hated dolls from the time she was a little kid) vied for space with an inflatable child's swimming pool filled with rubber ducks. Model trains whizzed around the room. At least early on, an entire wall was devoted exclusively to pictures of Nancy Reagan, who was pretty much Jodie's antithesis, both socially and politically. Somehow having Nancy leering at her with that famous frozen smile was a reminder to be true to herself no matter how rich and famous she got. Of course, later when Jodie's and the Reagans' lives crossed in such a horrifying way, the pictures were removed without comment by Hutman.

It was an out-and-out rejection of the ultratasteful house on Cahuenga. Jodie had shared her room there for many years with Connie and Cindy, and even after they moved out, she'd never tried to put her imprint on it. There was a bed, a pair of dressers, lots of books, and Jodie. No posters, no shelf full of stuffed animals, nothing that would have made her room unsuitable for display on a decorator's tour.

Jodie has often said that her first apartment was the happiest, most civilized home she ever had. It was her own, a place marked with her own identity, a place where she could have friends over who didn't have to meet Mom's strict standards. Finally she was experiencing at least part of the idealized collegiate life she had dreamed of. At family gatherings she would proudly display pictures of it, while Mom blanched as the rest of us admired the Nancy wall.

Despite her sizable earnings from her fourteen films, touching the trust funds was strictly forbidden. They were generating enough money to pay for college and look after Mom, and that was it. The capital had to be preserved in case Jodie decided never to act again. So she lived as frugally as any other student, getting by on about $30 per week after the rent and board was paid. (One ironic note, though: while at Yale she took a quick trip to Japan to make a Toyota ad, which paid a cool million dollars.) There was a barbecue in a small yard and regularly home-cooked meals for groups of friends. During cold, snowy New England winter days, huge pots of soup boiled on the stove (her favorites were, and still are, watercress, lentil, and sweet potato), which Jodie would freeze in individual serving-size containers.

The circle of friends she cooked for at Yale became close, dear friends. Fifteen years later they still form her inner circle. Randy Stone has become a film producer himself, David Duchovny is star of *The X-Files*, and Marco Pasanella is a furniture designer whose sideways rocker was bought by President Clinton (and whose design taste even Mom likes).

One of the strict requirements for being a friend of Jodie's is that you can't be in awe of her and must have the guts to say shut up when she prattles on. She has many acquaintances and values them, but newcomers are rarely allowed into that inner circle ("I have very, very few friends," Jodie says). In recent years she has become close to a few more movie people, but, curiously, almost none of them are actors; they are technicians who have worked on her films.

"I don't really hang around actors," she says with a genuine distaste that harkens back to Mom's frequent put-downs of actors as "dumb and uneducated." "Actor personalities, those people who do imitations all the time—

I hate that, it drives me crazy. The people who do accents all the time, who sort of sing all the time. I hate that."

If Jodie dislikes overly theatrical types, she truly loathes Hollywood phonies. One of her favorite sports is exposing them. When she smells phoniness in the air, she sometimes will start prattling on about something she knows nothing about, say rocket science. She'll make up terminology and launch into an impossibly detailed description of something that is wholly imaginary. If the intended victim nods knowingly and pretends to understand what she's talking about, she'll run with the charade, laughing to herself all the while, or maybe getting a friend like Randy Stone to join in. She never exposes her victims, though; it's enough for her that she knows. Her refusal to suffer fools gladly reminds me a lot of Dad. Jodie doesn't know it, because she refuses all acquaintance with him, but they actually have quite a few traits in common, particularly their intelligence.

A variety of minor injustices also drive Jodie up the wall. One of them is that rock stars are made into instant movie stars and paid millions to "pretend" to act. She is quick to point out that she has invested thirty years of dues paying in the film business. A rumor that Sting was being cast as Picasso (a far-out bit of Hollywood silliness that never came to pass) was particularly grating.

Another of her pet peeves is the renowned Polo Lounge in the Beverly Hills Hotel, where Hollywood moguls meet to power-lunch. She frequently compares the frontline troops of the movie business, who are in the trenches every morning at six, usually on some wretched out-back location, with the "suits," the lawyers and money men she invariably refers to as "the idiots in the Polo Lounge."

When her friends bonded with her at Yale, Jodie was not acting, looking, or feeling like a celebrity, so it was easier for them not to be dazzled by her presence. Now, though she does not seek out fame, she is inevitably touched by the aura of glamour that surrounded her arrival at Rex Restaurant after winning the Oscar for *Silence*.

"When I was at Yale," she recalled, "my career wasn't going that well, so I didn't feel like a movie star. College was a very pure place. It was a place where I got to figure out things I never would have been able to figure out anywhere else."

After growing up in Mom's *Architectural Digest*–inspired houses, where almost everything was too precious to touch, Jodie needed to live with miscellany in college. Ten years later, despite all her riches, she is still that way. She lived for a long time with little more than a big-screen TV and a bed in her house in Los Angeles. The important room to Jodie is the kitchen, where she has mastered the culinary techniques she started at Yale. Her Williams-Sonoma gourmet kitchen equipment catalogue is dog-eared and always near the phone. Her food tastes still aren't fancy; she favors a few well-chosen ingredients in a dish, happy with an honest-to-goodness tomato and a splash of vinegar instead of slices of foie gras in an exotic coulis.

For the first three years at Yale, Jodie made no feature films—save for the 1983 made-for-TV movie *Svengali* with Peter O'Toole. It was not a great hit, though critics praised the chemistry between the two stars. The film, a third remake of the famous George du Maurier novel *Trilby*, in which a singer falls under the hypnotic spell of her manager, was shot on location in New York during the winter of 1982.

Jodie commuted almost daily by train from New Haven to New York, keeping up with her schoolwork by studying between takes and on the train.

Gossip wags in New York gasped when Jodie and O'Toole were spotted holding hands as they strolled around Manhattan. The breathless talk was that Jodie, just turned twenty, had fallen under the hypnotic spell of the forty-nine-year-old O'Toole. It was pointed out that the randy English actor had a history of cradle-robbing and had been recently divorced.

Jodie, as usual, refused to say anything, but O'Toole, apparently flattered, waxed poetic: "I keep an open mind and an open pair of arms. There is nothing on earth as good as a man and a woman."

During the summer of 1982 Jodie had signed on for yet another TV movie, this one a knock-off of *Topper*, called *O'Hara's Wife*. Ed Asner starred as a businessman whose dead wife, played by Mariette Hartley, returns as a ghost to help him out. As in *Topper*, she is visible only to him. Jodie played the couple's daughter, trying hard to find some humor in the role. "Forgettable" and "trite" were words critics used to sum up the picture.

This was a transition period in her career. During those years she had trouble finding good vehicles. She became very discouraged and on many days was close to packing it in. "There I was at nineteen or twenty years old thinking, 'What's this? What am I doing?' I'm going to some rotten audition with a miniskirt on, and I twirl around for some guy to say, 'Well, you know your ass is too big.' And then go to the next one? It's like, 'This is my mission in life?' And so I got really depressed." But Jodie's friends, like John Hutman, had faith she would survive yet another series of blows and come out better than ever.

Mom, in particular, was there for Jodie. She would spend hours at a time on the phone with her, talking to Jodie and offering support, listening to Jodie and extending sympathy. I still remember how difficult it was to get hold of Mom in those days: the busy signals lasted for hours.

"Child actors are more fragile than the rest of us," says Martin Scorsese, "because they do not have normal child-hoods. And for that reason, many of them hit those depths of despair when they get older. And Jodie has been able to weather all that. The more adversity she had, the better she came through."

During Christmas of 1983 our whole family went to Europe to vacation and watch her work. It gave me a first-hand look at how consumed she had become with her career. From our various locations we all flew into Barcelona, Spain, and stayed in a seaside villa in the town of Cadaques. It was the first time in several years we had a chance to be together for an extended time, so there was a great deal of tentative reaching out to get to know each other again.

Mom was on top of her game, certainly the happiest she had ever been, basking in her youngest daughter's fame and wealth. She had reached several goals only dreamed of wist-fully back at that Catholic boarding school in Milwaukee. Adding to that was the fact that she was unencumbered; for the first time in her life she had no one to answer to, no one to take care of. Mom was certainly happy to have her brood together in such a posh setting and was as loving, but prickly, as she had ever been.

I was sober and in the process of finalizing my divorce

from my wife Diana. That marriage had been tumultuous from the start and ended with a shock. Still in love, though living together was an impossibility, we had a for-old-times-sake fling before parting. Just before leaving for Europe, Diana gave me the news she was pregnant. Our second son, Bryce Killian Foster, was the result. I sighed and vowed that I would try my best to be a good father to him.

My sisters and I were still licking our considerable wounds, and initially, the reunion seemed more like a gathering of survivors from some sort of natural disaster than a family reunion. As a result we at first tended to tiptoe around each other. After a few days the old closeness, the rollicking pillow-fight family atmosphere, was comfortably back.

It was great to see Connie. We've always had a great relationship, and she has always been the family member any of us can turn to in times of trouble. She seemed her usual cheerful, level-headed self, but her husband was going through some serious problems with alcohol and cocaine abuse, and life was not all rosy for her. As ever, she was our peacemaker, able to see everyone's point of view. She had her son Christian with her, who played with Cindy's son Alexander.

Cindy had been living in France since 1978. The bad crowd she'd fallen in with while we were teenagers had led her through some pretty harrowing times. Cindy had overcome the worst of her emotional problems and alcohol abuse, in part by moving to France and getting away from the influences—including our family—that had pushed her so close to the edge. Paris had been good to Cindy; she was married, teaching English, and happy with her life. Despite our tempestuous relationship as children, she and I got along well. She was, however, still capable of remembering the most embarrassing possible incident from the faraway past, and gleefully broadcasting it in a crowded three-star restaurant.

Most transformed and evolved was Jodie. She had weathered a crisis—which none of us dared to mention—and was coming into her own as an actress and a person. Gone was the relatively passive actress who simply showed up for work and hit the mark. In the film she was making, my little sister was pushing for script changes, chatting, and cajoling in three languages nearly the entire time we were together.

The two of us really connected on a brilliantly cloudless day when the Mediterranean was like the blue of Paul Newman's eyes. Jodie and I woke early, got Connie's little boy Christian and Cindy's Alexander in their bathing suits, grabbed a huge blue raft, and ran down to the sea.

The drop ten feet out from the shoreline was precipitous, thirty feet or so, and the water was calm as a lake. The children were naturally scared at first but once assured they were safe, they started to enjoy themselves. Leaning over the edge of the raft was like gazing into another world. The crystal-clear water was teeming with all manner of marine life.

I remember thinking that I had never seen Jodie as playful and fun. She was splashing, giggling like a schoolgirl, and being as silly as she pleased, making our nephews ecstatic. There were few times even during her childhood that she was carefree. Jodie always had her eyes on the prize. It seemed almost that she was trying to teach herself to have fun. Sure enough, as soon as the day was over, she was all business again.

Unfortunately, we saw Jodie only on the weekends, when she would jet down from France. And even then she was occupied with business much of the time. When we sat together for meals, she seemed distracted, not interested in the reminiscences or the minibattles. It seemed she had nothing in common with the rest of us. Work provided the perfect excuse for escaping her family.

She finally thawed out as work on her film began to wind down. We went to the family apartment in Paris, and there Jodie began to show a little of the camaraderie that we'd once shared. One of the first nonfamily members to drop by was a well-known, sex-siren starlet who was a close friend of Jodie's. To my surprise, Jodie mischievously eyed me after the visit and said, "Hey, Bud, she told me she's got the hots for you and wants to get it on."

I started to drool, and told her she had to get me together with the actress immediately. The vacation began to take on a whole different hue, distinctly undomestic. But Jodie quickly threw a bucket of cold water in my face. "She's got syphilis or something, I'm sure, Bud. The girl is Typhoid Mary. It's out of the question."

Watching this beauty slip through my fingers was terrible. During the weeks we spent in Paris, I was inconsolable. But Jodie was adamant that she was not going to let me get anywhere near her. I babbled on about condoms and penicillin. Jodie only laughed and shook her head.

The film she was making, directed by Claude Chabrol, was based on Simone de Beauvoir's novel *The Blood of*

Others, a romantic story set in Paris and rural France just before World War II. In the U.S. it was shown as a six-hour miniseries on HBO, while in Europe the film was released under the title *Le sang des autres* and was shown theatrically.

Jodie and Michael Ontkean play the star-crossed lovers Helene and Jean, who must choose between their love and their country. "It's about the choice between love and war," Jodie said. "What a woman will do for a man, what a man will do for his country and what he won't do for a woman."

Claude Chabrol, one of the most venerated filmmakers in France, paid Jodie a high compliment during filming: "Jodie is a fascinating character, and I let her do her own thing," the director said. "She is so close to the character, very strong, very impulsive."

Nonetheless, *The Blood of Others* was the last movie she would make for three years, which was the longest fallow period since 1972, when she was nine. She was determined to wait for the right roles to come along, and though she had offers for all kinds of movies that might have brought a fast buck, none of them satisfied her. She was at an awkward age when most of the available parts called for cuteness or naivete. She wasn't interested. She had her standards, and she was going to stick to them.

While we were in Paris, Jodie was sharing her one-bedroom apartment with a woman about ten years older, a fashion-accessory designer and businesswoman from Los Angeles. They clearly had a serious relationship. I thought nothing of that, but I was surprised that the woman acted so dominant. It's very unlike Jodie to be in any relationship where she does not have at least an equal hand. This woman seemed to

be completely setting Jodie's agenda for her, making decisions about ordering croissants for breakfast and what time
they went home at night.

Mom clearly approved and encouraged the friendship,
which was amusing to me, because if Jodie had been bossed
around by a male, Mom would have been outraged; since it
was a woman, it was okay. I thought maybe she was a substitute for when Mom couldn't be around. In fact, when I first
met the woman, I was surprised by how much she reminded
me of Aunt Jo. She had the same close cropped hair, square
jaw, and wore no makeup.

Years later both Jodie and Mom were sporting the
woman's fashion accessories, so I assume it was a long-term
relationship.

There have been rumors for years that Jodie is a lesbian,
rumors to which she has refused to respond. Part of her
refusal is that purposefully denying she's a lesbian would
seem to say that being gay is a bad thing, and she would
never want to give that impression. The other reason is
simply that Jodie guards all elements of her private life passionately and has a policy of never talking about them at all.
And that extends to talking to her family about her sexuality. It's a subject we would never speak about openly.
That's just the way the Foster family is and always has been.
I have always assumed Jodie was gay or bisexual, but I
wouldn't dare bring it up and risk incurring Mom's wrath.
It's a subject she is supertouchy about, to say the least.

Jodie has a sense of humor about all the rumors. When it
was whispered that she and Kelly McGillis, her costar from
The Accused, were having an affair, Jodie thought it was
hilarious, as did Kelly. Jodie told me she had spent one night

at Kelly's apartment because Kelly is a friend and was going through a hard time. She thought it pretty ridiculous that just because she had spent the night at someone's home, it was assumed she'd had sex with her.

A few years ago when a reporter noticed that Jodie and her *Nell* coproducer, Renee Missel, were wearing matching bracelets, much whispering was done. Both Jodie and Renee refused to answer any questions from the "curiosity machine," as Jodie calls the gossip press. The truth is that she gives everybody who works on a movie with her a present at the end of filming, and she wears it until she begins her next project. The bracelet was a *Little Man Tate* memento, and all the women associated with the movie got one.

But the rumor was typical of how closely Jodie is watched and how anxious the press is to label her. I've heard that one tabloid has a standing offer of $100,000 if a woman who has had an affair with Jodie will come forward with proof of it and tell all the gory details to the paper. In many stories published about her, even in quite respectable magazines, the writers make a point of mentioning that Jodie refuses to discuss her love life and her "inclinations," clearly implying that those inclinations are toward homosexuality.

"I don't talk about my private life, and that's probably why I'm sane," Jodie says without a trace of irony.

Those who wish to believe that Jodie is gay have tried to substantiate their theory by pointing to her brief love scene with Nastassja Kinski in *Hotel New Hampshire* and a scene in which she flirts with two lesbian characters in *Carny*. But that's as illogical as suggesting that she has something in common with the homicidal girl in *The Little Girl Who Lives Down the Lane*. Besides, as bossy as Jodie may be on the set, it doesn't make sense that she would try to rewrite scripts so she can drop hints that she's gay.

In 1991 when *Silence of the Lambs* was released, militant gay groups attacked her viciously because the serial killer in the film was portrayed as an effeminate, gay transvestite, though Jodie was neither the director nor the writer. One particularly virulent publication plastered posters of Jodie all over New York City bearing the words ABSOLUTELY QUEER. Jodie's sexual persuasion thus became a topic for gossip and discussion in periodicals such as the *Village Voice*, in which screenwriter Cindy Carr took her tormentors to task. Through it all, Jodie maintained a stoic silence, sticking with one of her main tenets of faith, which is never to willingly let anyone else dictate the terms of her life.

If you subscribe to the stupid theory that all lesbians hate men, you could argue that Mom's attitude toward men could have swayed Jodie in that direction. Also, we were partially raised by a lesbian. But I think the net effect of our upbringing was to make all of us kids more tolerant and open-minded. (Ironically, I am certain that Mom, of all people, wouldn't tolerate Jodie having an openly lesbian relationship, out of fear it would negatively impact her career.)

To be sure, men in Jodie's life have not been exemplary. Our father let her down, and eventually I let her down, too, by bailing out of the family and screwing up my life. But I know that she has never adopted the bitterness about men expressed so often by our mother.

She learned on her own there were men who could fulfill her needs. Jodie has had love affairs with men all her life. She was sexually knowledgeable at a young age and has had an active love life. In addition to the young French soldier she met in Tahiti, she dated a tennis player for several years and had a passionate relationship with him. And according to Mom, she had a serious relationship with English actor Julian Sands while they worked together on the film *Siesta*.

Briefly, I held out hope she would marry Sands, who was recently divorced and had a small child. He seemed perfect for her, and it appeared to me she desperately needed the equilibrium marriage can bring. But Jodie was ambivalent, unprepared to consider the issue. She was in her twenties and struggling to get her adult career on track. Sands, while apparently smitten with her both emotionally and intellectually, finally gave up on Jodie.

People also don't consider that Jodie learned early on to be extremely guarded about her love life. As a teenager, Mom heaped such criticism on Jodie whenever she brought a potential boyfriend home that she stopped doing it entirely. All of us did, for that matter. Now that the whole world gossips about her, Jodie is even more private. Because she doesn't flaunt her love life like Madonna or Sharon Stone, people whisper she must be a lesbian.

The persistent rumors and even the blatant so-called "outing" of Jodie by a gay magazine sometimes hang in the air like a bitter odor at family gatherings. But as in almost all matters with my family, the subject is never addressed. I remember once Mom called me and said, "Buddy, I have good news. Your sister is pregnant." For some reason I thought she meant Jodie and expressed my shock. Mom said, "Obviously I mean Cindy." But I had crossed an invisible line, had violated some secret pact. She was embarrassed, and so was I. The conversation, concerning what should have been joyful news, ended badly.

Jodie has always been a very solitary person, and she likes it that way. The fact that she prefers to live alone, that she doesn't go to Hollywood parties and premieres if she can possibly avoid them, gives some people reason to assume that she is hiding something, like a girlfriend. They forget how badly she was burned by being the focus of someone else's fantasies. I also sometimes wonder if Hinckley's threats against any man who might have stood between them don't still linger in Jodie's mind. Why make it clear that she loves one man in particular when some nut job out there might decide to eliminate a rival?

It's important to understand that if Jodie has to pay the price of fame to do the work she loves and feels is important, she will do it on her own terms. One of the rare satisfactions Jodie enjoys from attention is seeming an enigma. She loved it as a little girl, when her deep voice and quick mind caused adults to do a doubletake, and she loves it now. In an interview with *Rolling Stone* she once said, "I have this fascination with public personae and private people. There's that juxtaposition of image versus intimacy."

Jodie is content to let people whisper all they want about her, as long as they don't know what they are talking about.

TEN

There is nothing more comfortable to me than being in front of a camera.
　　　　　　　—JODIE FOSTER

The three or four years after graduating from Yale were the hardest of my sister's life. She has often said she would hate to have to relive her early twenties. Struggling to regain a sense of where she was going and what the future was going to hold, Jodie made no movies from 1984 to 1986.

During this troubled time she had an unusual lapse of judgment. On her return from our family holiday in Spain and Paris, she was charged with the possession of a small amount of cocaine. Those of us who had just been with her were mystified. Jodie seemed to have recovered her equilibrium in every way possible: her weight was down, her grades were outstanding again, and her spirits appeared thoroughly revived.

But on her reentry to the United States at Boston's

Logan Airport, agents found a gram of cocaine in Jodie's purse, according to their official report. She was held for several hours while U.S. Customs inspectors debated what to do with her. Out of either sympathy for what she had been through two years earlier, or ineptness, depending upon your point of view, they told her if she paid a $100 administrative fine on the spot, they would forget the incident.

Naturally, she handed over the money in a flash, and with a great sigh of relief she dashed off for a Los Angeles–bound flight. For a brief time she held out hope her lapse would go unnoticed by the public—and more important—by Mom. But that was not to be. Several days later, when Suffolk County District Attorney Newman Flanagan learned of the arrest and summary dismissal, he saw political gold. He thundered: "How can we arrest people on the streets of Boston and ignore Logan Airport?"

Furious at missing a chance to bust a movie star, the authorities went to an East Boston district court magistrate and requested that a summons be issued ordering her to return to Boston the following month. That would give them plenty of time to get word out of a genuine show trial, where, in the glare of TV cameras and flashing bulbs, Jodie would have to answer charges that could lead to a year-long prison sentence.

All the grandstanding garnered plenty of publicity, and Mom, the one person Jodie hoped wouldn't learn of her indiscretion, watched the news with horror and outrage. Characteristically, she saw the incident as the death knell of the career she had struggled so mightily to beget. The perfect porcelain princess had finally shown a flaw.

When the tears and recriminations were over, though,

Mom proved to be as astute and loyal as ever. She hired a crack attorney who arranged for a closed-door hearing. The matter was quietly settled and most of the damage controlled.

Yet the publicity hounds had not yet extracted their pound of flesh. Reporters called Yale administrators to report the news and ask for the university's comment on the situation, as though there was any comment the school could reasonably be expected to make. Thankfully, the imbroglio passed without any administrative action. In subsequent years Jodie has never had even a hint of a problem with drugs, so the scare may have been for the best.

Academics, like almost everything else, came very easy to Jodie. Despite her troubled first year at Yale and disruptions for work over the next several semesters, she breezed through the challenging program. In 1984, she received a bachelor's degree in literature, specializing in African-American literature and (just about making Mom's heart burst with pride) graduating magna cum laude. Her senior thesis was on the black feminist writer Toni Morrison.

The achievement was more notable because a year before her 1985 graduation, Jodie had gone back to work with a vengeance, trying to force the notoriety of the Hinckley horrors to fade and to get her career back on track. Her first film was *Hotel New Hampshire*, written and directed by Tony Richardson (of *Tom Jones* fame), who did an excellent job adapting the complex, picaresque John Irving novel. The film, which was shot during a bitterly cold winter in Montreal, is the story of an eccentric, ill-fated family that runs hotels in various exotic locales like Vienna, and along the way adopts a cast of bizarre characters, each of whom seems a metaphor for something or other. They include a girl (Nastassja Kinski) who will only go out in public dressed as a bear, a cabal of crazed anarchists, a voluptuous waitress, a little girl who can't (physically) grow up, and a dead dog named Sorrow, who always shows up when tragedy is in the wind.

New Hampshire was the first of a string of films in which Jodie played a victim. Her character, Franny Berry, is gang-raped early in the film and deals with her pain throughout. Jodie's character also has a lustful relationship with her brother (Rob Lowe) that is consummated with vigor. The film, starring Beau Bridges as the father, is a seriocomic sleigh ride through a dozen vignettes that should be totally implausible but somehow make sense. Jodie summed up *New Hampshire* as "a juxtaposition of the incredible and mundane."

Ironically, probably because of the Hinckley nightmare and the avalanche of unwanted publicity, Jodie was offered her highest fee ever to make *New Hampshire*, $500,000, despite her stalled career. Once she had time to heal from the Hinckley ordeal, even Jodie found a positive side to it—it made her stronger. "I don't understand derangement. I do understand survival. Faced with death, I would survive." But the fact that it made her worth vastly more money at the box office was one of those unspeakable ironies at which you can only shake your head, which is what Jodie did.

The reviews for the film were good, and it seemed the adult phase of her career was taking off. But that wasn't to be the case. The transition from Yale back to the real world, and Hollywood, was far more difficult than she imagined.

The day after graduation, Jodie took on the melancholy job of closing up the cozy little apartment she had shared for nearly three years with her best friend, John Hutman. Packing away the model trains and various oddities was a near-tearful task. There were sad farewells to all her friends. Reflecting years later on her college days, Jodie said she felt the experience had saved her career. Adopting a goal that had nothing to do with acting had prevented her from sinking into the morass that all too often ruins the lives of child actors. Instead, she was able to gain a perspective on a way of life far removed from TV and movie studios.

Upon graduation, however, she had to plunge back into that world. She found a small apartment near the West Hollywood area where we had spent most of our early years and basically asked herself, "What now?"

In the four years she had been away, the town was much changed. Traffic was worse, favorite restaurants like the drive-in Stan's on Sunset Boulevard, with its roller-skating waiters and garish fifties neon, which we had gone to since we were little kids, had been razed, and the renowned "laid back" California manner had been replaced by a far more frantic style.

Many neighborhoods that had once teemed with happy children riding bikes and climbing trees were now full of abandoned buildings, sprayed with gang graffiti and boarded-up windows. Kids no longer necked in cars parked high up on Mulholland Drive because of the explosion of rapes and murders in the area. Quiet communities where we had played had been bulldozed and replaced with huge shopping centers and buildings like the cavernous abomination called the Blue Whale, containing the Pacific Design Center (which Mom found to be a paradise of wildly expensive home furnishing).

Jodie did not take the changes well. "After I graduated, I went back to Los Angeles and got depressed and never left my house," she said. The disruption and decay of the old order was a metaphor for her life. "I was just scared, scared of what was going to come next."

During this period Jodie fought off depression and mostly spent her time alone. Long hours were spent sitting in dark theaters watching the foreign-language movies she loves, or at home reading.

Everything had changed. The house was gone, our whole family had scattered for good, and Jodie knew she didn't want to be Mommie's little girl anymore. Mom was there for Jodie, always ready to lend an ear and provide advice, but it wasn't the same. Jodie had grown up and Mom couldn't shelter her anymore.

In the midst of this low time our grandmother died. Growing up, we had only one visit that I can recall from our Grandmother Lucy Schmidt, the woman who raised Mom. She came to California in 1967, just after we had moved back into the city from the beach. It was a wonderful two weeks and I was always sorry she never returned.

Grandma Lucy was a big, heavy-set woman who was full of love. One thing about her that tickled us was her penchant for scolding Mom. Of course, our mother was undisputed queen of the house and ruled with an iron fist, so we were delighted to see her knocked off the throne, if only for two weeks. I remember one particular stunt four-year-old Jodie did that set Mom off. Mom grabbed Jodie by the arm, shook her, threw her into her room, then yelled and screamed. For us it was standard procedure, nothing remarkable.

But Grandmom was very upset at the harshness of the punishment. She got right in Mom's face, wagged her finger, and said, "Don't you ever talk to your kids that way. I don't ever want to hear you use foul language in their presence. That's absolutely wrong, Evelyn." Mom was so stunned she actually apologized to Jodie. The rest of us could barely restrain ourselves from bursting into laughter. It was the first time we had ever seen Mom back down.

Grandma Lucy returned to Rockford, Illinois, and I never saw her again. In her later years she lived alone and was very involved with church activities such as bingo games, church socials, and bake sales. Sadly, her last days were painful and ghastly. All her life she had suffered from severe diabetes and had to inject herself with insulin daily. For years she battled the disease with medicine, prayer, and sheer willpower. But in the end the diabetes caused irreparable damage to her blood vessels, and gangrene developed in her legs. During the winter of 1985, Mom went to Rockford to be with her.

As soon as she arrived, she realized Grandma was even worse than anticipated. Mom was horrified when the doctors told them the only hope was to amputate both her legs. Though they'd had little contact, Lucy never spoke a word of recrimination and instantly established a rapport with Mom.

The thought of this dear, sweet, old woman going through such an operation was beyond imagining. But Grandmom decided she would let the doctors do what they thought was necessary and continue fighting for her life.

As she was wheeled into the operating room, Mom held

Grandma's hand for support, tears coursing down their faces. Grandma Lucy just smiled broadly and confidently, her faith still fully intact.

During the operation, Mom stayed close and struggled to be as brave as Grandmom. Against all odds, considering her weakened heart and advanced years, she survived the operation itself. But several days later, at age eighty-eight, she succumbed to heart failure.

Mom was deeply affected. For Mom, her stepmother's death severed the last link to her roots, to her biological family back in Brooklyn that was too shamed by her accidental conception to keep her. It meant saying good-bye to the mother who had shaped her personality with a rigid set of Midwestern standards. And it was a reminder that she was no longer a teenage girl who had run off to Hollywood, for Mom was now about to turn fifty-seven.

I have always regretted the fact we didn't spend more time with Grandma. Whenever I asked why we didn't go to see her, I was given any of a half dozen excuses. She was sick, she was busy, or she didn't want to be bothered. Despite her conflicts with Grandma, Mom was careful not to vent her frustration in front of us the way she did about Dad. That made it possible to idealize Lucy in a way, and it breaks my heart to find out, all these years later, how lonely she was.

Grandmom Lucy's death hit Jodie hard as well. Later she said morosely, "It made me feel I should never love unhesitantly again. I guess all of us have felt that way when a grandparent passes away." That may seem overly dramatic, given how little contact there had been between them. But I think it reflects how susceptible Jodie was to despair at the time, as well as the depth of feeling that Grandmom Lucy was able to inspire.

In the time following Grandmom Lucy's death, things were exceedingly dismal for Jodie, not just personally but professionally. The scripts she was offered were terrible, and the ones she really wanted were given to other actresses. To her credit, Jodie felt strongly that she should do nothing rather than make movies that were embarrassments. Pressure from her agents and other advisers to accept something grew very strong, which of course only increased her anxiety level. Mom felt she should at least make a small, arty movie, if nothing else, just to keep her name out there. She was beginning to be thought of by some as a novelty act: the teenage hooker in *Taxi Driver* who was stalked by the nut who shot Reagan.

Finally, in 1986, Jodie began to act again. The next five movies were not great, and a few, arguably, should never have been made. But she had to do something, anything, to get her career moving. At least, she was back on the movie set, where she is happiest.

In 1986 Jodie went to New Zealand to make a film called *Mesmerized*, costarring John Lithgow. It was a murky, gothic period piece in which she plays another victim, this time an innocent orphan who marries a dour older man and plans his demise when he proves abusive. One critic dismissed the movie, calling it "an embarrassing hash of horror."

The next movie was worse. *Siesta*, released in 1987, was a film with a brilliant script that was far ahead of its time. Pat Lefkowitz's work reminded me strongly of Salman Rushdie's *Satanic Verses*. Unfortunately, the script did not translate well to the screen. Directed by Mary Lambert, who is best known for her Madonna music videos, *Siesta* starred Ellen Barkin, Martin Sheen, Isabella Rossellini, and Julian Sands. Barkin, improbably, skydives into Spain and endures a bizarre ordeal involving murder and a would-be rapist, a cab driver with rusty teeth. Jodie has a mercifully brief role as a snooty socialite, displaying a passable British accent, and has a love scene with Julian Sands. *Siesta* was almost universally panned; one of the kindest critiques called the film "incomprehensible."

Next was *Five Corners*, which was critically praised though not a box-office smash. Based on a script by *Moonstruck* writer John Patrick Shanley, it starred John Turturro as a deranged but sympathetic loser who stalks and attempts to force himself on Jodie. He turns violent when spurned, knocks her out, and carries her draped over his shoulder like a sack of potatoes for the rest of the flick. "It wasn't exactly the juiciest role. I'm unconscious throughout most of the movie," Jodie laughed.

Critics marveled at her choice of a role in which she plays a stalker victim so soon after Hinckley, as though it was accidental. I think it was a necessary step in the slow, therapeutic process of closure for her. *Daily Variety* said Jodie "was serviceable, but a little out of her element as a tough Catholic kid."

But *Stealing Home*, also made in 1988, reminded people just how good Jodie could be with the right material. The body of the film is a series of flashbacks to the fifties and sixties, since it begins with news of her character Katie's suicide, which sets the plot in motion. Mark Harmon plays the adult Billy Wyatt, a baseball-obsessed youngster she baby-sat and forever influenced with her rebelliousness, free spirit, and finally lovemaking.

Having drifted aimlessly since Katie went away, Harmon's character, a talented but failed baseball player at thirty-eight, finally finds himself after she dies. The film is heartbreaking and bittersweet without veering into the maudlin. Once again Jodie portrayed a casualty, this time of her own grief. And again her character was a blue-collar underdog who is pushed aside by society, a theme that remains an important part of her art and philosophy.

Jodie loved the script from the beginning. "It talks about the things that affect you indelibly, places you've been, circumstances, heroes, unresolved emotions. I also love the idea that there's a hero for you, and that hero, for a lot of men, is a woman. There aren't a lot of those. But mostly, it was just that she was real—she's bratty, she smokes, she does things that aren't admirable. But she's real."

When Billy Wyatt is about ten years old, Katie gives him a typically cockeyed piece of advice. "Girls like guys who smoke. Let's smoke."

Jodie's performance in *Stealing Home* was praised as "unforgettable." Though the film was not commercial enough to provide the fire her career really needed, Jodie had succeeded in making a name for herself as a mature actress. It was apparent to the deal makers she could dazzle with the right material. For her efforts she had a few million in the bank and was once again a player in Hollywood, somebody whose phone call is taken. Now all that remained was finding the right part to cement her gains.

Unfortunately, her return to the limelight also meant exposure to creeps. Life for celebrated people in the United States had become dangerous. John Lennon had been shot to death, George Harrison was shadowed and threatened, a psycho broke into Rod Stewart's Holmby Hills mansion and physically attacked him. Cher and Olivia Newton-John and dozens of others were threatened or injured by deranged fans. Led by top security consultant Gavin DeBecker and others, an entire industry devoted to protecting the rich and famous came into being. Jodie would require a great deal of their services.

Each time Jodie had a movie released or made public appearances, the threats started again, as constant as clockwork. The perpetual fear that Jodie felt was something she was going to have to live with for the rest of her life; constant vigilance was going to be required.

Fear of crazies drastically altered her lifestyle, making Jodie one of the most security-conscious celebrities in Hollywood. She has struggled to adopt the positive attitude that Hinckley and the other nut were flukes, and that the odds of it happening to her again are remote, but every stranger's face has the power to send a chill up her spine. Fan mail was forever banished from her presence, and several layers of screening protected her from possible threatening or weird phone calls.

Today some people have the number of her production office, though it is unlisted. Other, closer associates have Mom's number. A handful can reach her answering service. But virtually no one can pick up the phone and get Jodie on the line; she regards telephones as warily as a rattlesnake. People who know her never call at home even if they know the number, because she simply doesn't like to take phone calls at home and never discusses business there.

Thanks to some political connections, she is on a short

list of celebrities and politicians whose car license tags are computer keyed so that any attempt to run the tag and discover her home address triggers a police alert. And she has dark-tinted windows, protecting her from being easily recognized. Jodie's current home, a guest house on the estate of a legendary entertainer, is ringed with razor-sharp, electrified barbed wire and equipped with state-of-the-art alarms, including motion sensors and lasers. All the high-tech antiterrorist devices make her very uncomfortable. One of the least pretentious people ever to achieve fame, Jodie hates the trappings and the loss of freedom that come with it. While she is hiding behind the best security money can buy, she often feels like a prisoner.

When she was searching for office space for her Egg Pictures Company, her main concern was security. An armed guard waits outside her door around the clock, and panic buttons to call the police are everywhere. Whenever she tells anybody about her offices, the first thing she comments on is not the great views or the beautifully decorated rooms—designed by our sister Connie, with huge white couches and exquisitely painful black-and-white photographs—but the speed with which the guards respond to a summons. She is more determined than ever not to be a victim ever again.

As cautious as Jodie is, Mom still worries greatly about her. She says Jodie is naive to think she can walk the streets of Los Angeles or New York and not be recognized instantly. And she still is appalled that Jodie once opened her door without knowing who was knocking. Such a simple act, so potentially dangerous, shows how much she wishes, at heart, for a freer life.

As much as I am in awe of her talent and achievements, she has told me she is jealous of my quiet life in northern Minnesota. Success came at such an early age that Jodie has only hazy recollections of a time when she wasn't famous. She would truly like to be a "normal person" for the first time in her life. But she knows it's too late. Greta Garbo issued her "I want to be left alone" plea at the age of thirty-six, when she was just two years older than Jodie is at this writing, and Garbo was hounded to the day she died. In fact, tabloid scandal sheets all over the world gleefully published a picture of the star leaving her apartment for the last time, en route to a hospital to die. Her wretched condition and the look of horror in her eyes at being photographed that way make any decent person wince and turn away from the page.

Jodie has survived her horrible experiences with a rarely shaken poise and strength that has never involved the advice of entities from ancient Persia or appearances on *Geraldo* to blame everything on Mom or Dad or Satan. Ironically, she has done it by binding herself up in the very thing that has brought her so much of her grief: her career. The only thing I can imagine now that would truly threaten her is the loss of that same career. Because of what it can allow her to do, it is the thing that matters more to her than anything else.

ELEVEN

Truth is what I look for in a film, and the truth in female history is that it includes a lot of victimization.
—JODIE FOSTER

odie insists on giving a hundred and fifty percent when she does a film. She also believes that movies, like all worthy art, if done properly, should change people's lives. That is her goal every time she goes behind the camera or in front of it. "If I say yes to a picture, it's because I want to die for it," she's often said. For Jodie to love a movie, it has to follow her personal philosophy and reflect her values. The aim is for brutal—if need be—honesty. And her work has to teach a moral lesson: show that a strong, brave woman who refuses to capitulate will triumph in the end.

The directing she now does suits her ambitions and her personality because she is so decisive and willful, which is what it takes to make a movie: the ability to make sharp, clear judgments.

Jodie likes acting for the opposite reason: instead of being in control, she can release that control. Being emotional comes very hard for her. She couldn't afford to be emotional as a child and still be the sane one in the house. She learned to be almost totally cerebral and self-contained. As a result, she often keeps her anger and frustration inside, simmering until she's ready to explode, then she'll shout and scream. Acting draws her out and frees her to release the suppressed anger and frustration. She would probably get ulcers if she didn't play characters who are completely different from herself.

Jodie has long complained, with a touch of bitterness, about Mom's choices of early film roles for her. She has often said she would have picked different projects in some cases. But the disagreement didn't cause her to put her foot down until the early nineties, when she pushed Mom into a well-deserved, if reluctant, retirement. Only at that point could Jodie afford to be as choosy as she wanted.

In an ideal world, Jodie would have played only characters who take charge and make a difference. She now says emphatically that she did not want to play so many victims and was resentful that most of the roles available for a young, vulnerable-looking girl involved "running around in panties being chased by the monster," as she put it.

From her earliest memorable roles (the young hooker in *Taxi Driver*, the mischievous vixen in *Alice Doesn't Live Here Anymore*, and her "shockingly mature" portrayal of the homicidal girl in *The Little Girl Who Lives Down the Lane*) Jodie played the world-weary woman inside a child's body. She claims the roles were chosen by Mom, who insisted, and still argues, that each represented a good career move. Jodie sharply disagrees, saying the characters she played were a form of therapy for Mom. It seems fairly obvious to me that Mom was picking roles that featured an orphaned, or unwanted, or lost child struggling to survive on her wits against a sea of adult malfeasance.

Jodie feels Mom lived vicariously through her, watching characters act with strength and decisiveness—just the way Mom wished to be. Jodie feels cheated because what her characters say and do, and the message they convey about life and living, is so very important to her. Looking back at the films Mom chose for her, she is conflicted because it wasn't her play book she was following, it was another person's vision. "They were incredibly personal choices. She wanted those victims to survive," Jodie says.

A perfect example is *Alice Doesn't Live Here Anymore*, which was Jodie's first serious film. It is, in many ways, the world according to Brandy Foster. Ellen Burstyn's Alice character (for which she won the 1974 Best Actress Oscar) is a jazz singer, like Mom. She escapes from a bully of a husband who is killed in an auto accident (Mom always counselled us to think of Dad as dead). Men in the film are often leering and abusive. In one scene when Alice applies for a job as a saloon singer, the lecherous boss asks her to turn around, so he can ogle her derriere. "I don't sing with my ass," Alice snaps, a crack Mom surely appreciated. And finally there is the combative but ultimately loving relationship between Alice and her son. It has both the Sturm und Drang and the playful affection of our family life.

Ironically, the movie that most fits the monster metaphor that Jodie used to describe what she hated in movies is probably the first one on which she opposed Mom's advice and won. It was a part that, at first, Mom wanted nothing to do with, and it immediately followed *Alice.* In *Taxi Driver,* Jodie plays a sexually precocious teenage girl, often dressed very suggestively, who is the object of the attentions of the truly monstrous Travis Bickle. Bickle's gory shooting spree, in which he kills three men, is consummated with the intention of claiming Jodie's character from her clients and keepers.

The part was so appealing to Jodie because it was challenging, it represented a true step forward in her development, and because it was clearly an integral role in a serious movie that assembled a top-notch team. Yet Iris is a victim, and Jodie expressed no philosophical qualms about playing her.

Later the roles Jodie picked for herself began to feature a canny young woman who is in charge of the situation, who has simply to reason with the elders whose emotions betray them. In *Candleshoe,* she effortlessly divines the sundry deceptions that are taking place, from David Niven's many disguises to convince Helen Hayes she still has money, to the crooks' plot to steal the fortune Hayes doesn't know she still owns. In the end Jodie saves the bumbling good guys and trips up the wicked.

That was followed by *Foxes* and *Carny,* roles in which she was alternately wise beyond her years and seductive. *Foxes,* interestingly, featured a complex and stormy relationship between a mother, played by Sally Kellerman and Jodie's character, who was the more judicious and astute of the two by far. In *Carny* her two lovers, played by Gary Busey and Robbie Robertson, are swept away with their love for her. Again she herself is calm and in control, both in an emotional and a physical sense.

Jodie was able to see her roles in *Hotel New Hampshire,*
Mesmerized, Siesta, Five Corners, and *Stealing Home* as
somehow like this. This requires making some very fine distinctions and points out, in many ways and despite Jodie's
own feelings, that the difference between Mom's films and
Jodie's films isn't terribly great. The former do seem to
reflect Mom's childhood, when she was orphaned, rebel-
lious, and bitter at being shipped off to a convent without
her consent. Jodie's childhood was one in which there was a
vacuum of competent adult authority and control at times.
She was the one who was forced from the beginning to be
wise and in control. Rather than a polarity between Mom's
choices and Jodie's, there has been an evolution, one that
moved from simply getting revenge upon one's foes to
achieving a kind of transcendence over them and their
influence.

The contrast that best represents this evolution is
between *The Accused,* Jodie's 1988 movie, and *Hotel New
Hampshire.* In both films her character is raped. Unlike the
excruciating rape scene Jodie endured in *The Accused* four
years later, she opted to have a body double in *New Hampshire.* In an interview discussing that movie at the time of its
release, she said of her rape scene, "The actors who play
rapists have a hard time doing it because they are sensitive
and they know you like them. I don't think the guys would
have been able to do it if it had been me."

By the time of *The Accused,* she chided herself for having
a victim's response by feeling sorry for the *New Hampshire*
rapists in any way. She acted the rape scene in *The Accused*
herself, believing that the experience was crucial to what she
had to do. When the scene was finally finished, she was

bruised all over, as well as psychologically drained, but still found the strength and presence of mind to comfort the equally shaken men who played the rapists.

Jodie remembered thinking, "I don't want those guys to feel bad. I don't want them to feel guilty. And then a year later I said, 'What do I care?' It's a pretty strong feminine trait that it's okay for you to feel pain, but God forbid a man should cry. Whatever pain you go through, you must deserve it. That movie really made me examine that in myself."

Never had I seen Jodie as emotionally electrified, alternately wavering between exhilaration and despair, as she was during the making of *The Accused*. The project was clearly one that was going to bring out the best in her and take a heavy toll.

She called me to wish me a happy birthday very late one night from Canada, where the film was being shot. I could sense the tension in her voice in a way that alarmed me. During our conversation she said the tortures her character was going through reminded her in a very sad way of me and some of the trauma I had experienced.

But mostly I felt sorry for her. Jodie seemed cast adrift in a cauldron of frightening emotions: anger, rage, grief, and helplessness. I was sorry I couldn't reach across the thousands of miles between us and comfort her. After I mumbled inadequate reassurances, hung up, and headed back to bed, it occurred to me that Jodie had chosen to play out the rawest of human suffering for a living, and in some ways she was going to be a surrogate aching for her heroines as they struggled to triumph over life.

While Jodie was paying her career dues all over again in the late 1980s, I seemed to have finally gotten things together. Unfortunately, I was heading for another big crash. I didn't fall into a new round of addiction, but this new cycle did repeat many of the same mistakes I'd made before.

It all seemed so promising at the time. I was truly clean thanks to the Palmer program, and I spent a few years working as a counselor to other participants, gaining management responsibilities in the program. It was a relief and a blessing to be sober.

In 1985 I married again, confident that I was in control of my life. My second wife, Robin, was a counselor in a drug rehab program when we first met. I had demonstrated such control that I figured it was even time to enjoy life a little. I quit my job as a counselor and went into a new line of work where the money was better: auto sales. Man, I was hot. In just three months I became the top Volkswagen sales rep in California. Then I went to work for a Porsche dealer as sales manager: in six months we went from being twenty-sixth in sales nationwide to being number one. From there I went to Mercedes, the most prestigious car in the business.

The money was terrific, and it kept rolling in. My wife and I bought a big house, a couple of new cars, including one of those Mercedes. We had more credit cards than I could count. In fact, there was a lot that I wasn't counting, including the bills and the hours I was working.

Once again I was obsessed with providing for my family. My wife gave birth to a beautiful daughter, whom I named Courtney Jean in honor of Dad's sister. My older son, Lucius, was living with us, and if things went right, my other son, Bryce, might move in, too. I thought that as long as I was able to take care of them financially, everything would be all right.

It wasn't. My marriage began going down the toilet, and I worked more and more to avoid facing that fact. And the more I worked, the more I hated the work. I had dreams of being a hamster on a treadmill. I was back in the old trap of doing something I despised to satisfy other people.

One morning in 1988, I announced that I was going to quit selling cars. I wasn't going to do it that day, but the end was near. I didn't realize how near. When I came home for lunch that day, my wife was gone, and so was Courtney. In a phone call, my wife told me that there was nothing to hold our marriage together anymore, that I'd been a lousy father, and that I should forget about having anything to do with Courtney again.

As I rummaged through our papers, preparing for a divorce, I was overwhelmed by what I found. Our debts were staggering. Each credit card was charged to the limit; stacks of bills were late. The mortgage payment on the house, due regular as clockwork, was enormous. I couldn't stop working. I couldn't spend more time with my sons: without a step-mother in the house, Lucius would have to live with Diana again. As for Courtney, I wasn't sure I'd be able to see her at all. If there was any one point on which I had pinned my self-respect in the last few years, it was that I had been more of a father to my kids than my father had been to me. Now I was going to be reduced to being a weekend visitor.

In our dining room off of the living room was a small white table covered with a cloth. It seemed the perfect place to curl up and get away from everything. I crawled under it. What I didn't recognize then, since it had been painted and refinished so many times over the years, was that this was the same table I had hidden under during the storms of my childhood, including the day Aunt Jo stormed out of Mom's room with her derringer to confront Dad. Mom had kept it and lent it to me when we'd bought the house, and once again I was retreating there. Except this time I was the one with the gun: a .38 Smith & Wesson.

I have no recollection of those crucial moments, but somehow the huge blast when I pulled the trigger missed my head and my heart, instead blowing a hole in my upper left thigh, big enough to put a fist through. My son Lucius found me in a pool of blood, got help, and saved my life.

When I finally regained consciousness days later, Mom and the rest of my family (except Jodie, who was out of town) were standing by the hospital bed. Their concern was so different from my loneliness after the crash, and it was a telling sign of what was to come. On the phone, just about the first words out of Jodie's mouth were "I told you so," spoken with her compassionate, soft voice.

She had warned me against both of my marriages and had been aghast at the frenzied way I was working, borrowing and spending to buy cars, furniture, and tons of extraneous material things. The fact that my wife served me with divorce papers while I was in the intensive-care unit only reinforced Jodie's sense that she'd been right all along. I can't offer this as proof of her superior intellect: any fool could have seen it.

Lying on my back in the hospital, I realized that I had nowhere to go but up, and this time I was going to get some real help. My family got involved in my life for the first time since we were kids, and I welcomed it. Mom, bless her, paid half the huge attorney's fees of what proved to be a horrific divorce and child-custody battle, and I paid the rest over a period of years.

Even more important in the long run, a friend of mine at the Palmer drug abuse program referred me to psychiatrist George Blair, who had the skills and patience to help me find my way back from the wilderness. I was never billed for his services, which was a boon, because I had hardly enough money to get by. But I have often wondered if Jodie or Mom paid it, or if Dr. Blair just didn't bill me because he knew what dire straits I was in. Whoever paid, I love you and thank you.

The Accused, which earned Jodie her first Academy Award, gave her a chance to portray a character that resonated deeply within her. As soon as she read the script, she desperately wanted to play the role of the rape victim. She felt there was a starkness to the plot and the possibility for the portrayal of tremendous strength of character. Ironically, since it's now hard to imagine any other actress playing the role as well as Jodie did, she had to battle skeptical producers and agree to do a videotaped audition, like some rank amateur, to get the part.

At the time Jodie saw her show business career mostly in the past tense. She realized she had made five forgettable movies in a row, and since nothing of substance was being offered, she had no alternative but to make one last stand and try to get a good role, even if it meant making a fool of herself.

Her mentor Martin Scorsese warned her, in the kindest way possible, that she faced a bruising challenge to change

Jodie at age thirteen, about the time she did *Taxi Driver*, for which she was nominated for an Academy Award for best supporting actress. *Courtesy of Colin Dangaard.*

Jodie always bonded
with Aunt Jo. 1972.
Courtesy of Chris Hill.

Jodie during her martial arts training in 1973. She got
involved even more after the Hinkley assassination
attempt on President Reagan. *Courtesy of Chris Hill.*

Mom, Jodie, and
Cindy during a 1977
visit to see me in
"the hood."
Courtesy of Buddy Foster.

Connie, Jodie, and Cindy have stayed fairly close over the years. While I
was taking this photo, I'm sure they were thinking, "Hurry up so we can
beat the crap out of you!" *Courtesy of Buddy Foster.*

A rare occasion when we all were together at the same time for a picnic in Woodland Hills, California. *Courtesy of Buddy Foster.*

Jodie posing for big brother. *Courtesy of Buddy Foster.*

Jodie striking another pose.
1979.
Courtesy of Buddy Foster.

In the hospital after my tragic motorcross accident. *Courtesy of Buddy Foster.*

Our sister Lucinda at a family outing. *Courtesy of Buddy Foster.*

Mom and Dad during my wedding to Diana, 1978. This was a rare moment in getting them so close to each other. I remember Mom saying, "Smile, you bastard." *Courtesy of Buddy Foster.*

My first wife, Diana, and me with our son Lucius. *Courtesy of Buddy Foster.*

My children and me, 1994: Brice, Courtney, and Lucius V doing his grunge thing. *Courtesy of Buddy Foster.*

Our house in Hollywood in which Jodie was raised during her formative years. *Courtesy of Rochelle Law Wagener.*

Our father, Lucius, his current wife, Madeline, and their daughter, Luchan, who years later met Jodie at the *Little Man Tate* premiere for the kids in the state's program for gifted kids. *Courtesy of Buddy Foster.*

Jodie between takes during the filming of *Stealing Home*. *Courtesy of Angela Dito, Shooting Star.*

Jodie with Richard Burton, whom she and my mother greatly admired.
Courtesy of Mark Sennet, Shooting Star.

Jodie, right, and friends Natassia Kinski and Rob Lowe during filming of *The Hotel New Hampshire*. *Courtesy of Orion/Shooting Star.*

From left to right: Stacy (my wife) and me, Steve (friend of my sister Connie), Mom, Jodie, Christian (Connie's son), Connie, and Bob (Connie's husband) at the Rex during the Academy Awards–night party. *Courtesy of Buddy Foster.*

Jodie during the filming of *Carney*.   *Courtesy of Lorimar/Shooting Star.*

Jodie playing Clarice Starling in *Silence of the Lambs,* for which she won her second Academy Award.   *Courtesy of Orion/Shooting Star.*

Jodie doing *Nell*.   *Courtesy of 20th Century-Fox/Shooting Star.*

With my wife, Stacy in 1996. *Courtesy of Jeff Frey.*

Jodie got Mom's smile!   *Courtesy of Ron Davis/Shooting Star.*

the perception that Hollywood had of her of a sultry teen. But when she pulled it off, he was among the first to applaud.

"It is very, very hard for a child actor to gain acceptance in the world of mature, adult actors," Scorsese said. "Liz Taylor did it, but I can't think of too many others. But Jodie has certainly done it. She does it because it's all she does. She is very powerful."

The odds were certainly stacked against her. Whether Mom's remarks about the PLO in *Interview* magazine had anything to do with it or not, there was a great deal of hostility toward Jodie in Hollywood. Cruelly, it was said she had gone from nymphet to chubby college student, and no one was interested in her any longer.

Jonathan Kaplan, director of *The Accused*, wanted to give her a chance, but the producers were adamantly against it. They said she was too fat, and even said she wasn't "rapeable" enough. The implication was that the producers didn't feel Jodie was good-looking enough to make a gang of men want to rape her. Kaplan was forbidden to let her read the script or even to tell her where the auditions were being held.

But Kaplan had great admiration for her work and insisted she at least be given a chance. He later said, "It was obvious from the very first frame of the screen test that she was great in the role, but a factor that I think was in everybody's mind was the baggage she would bring to the role. Like the fact that she'd been through the whole Hinckley thing, that might be distracting for the audience. I didn't think it would."

When producers Stanley Jaffe and Sherry Lansing finally

relented and allowed Jodie to read for the part, she was clearly furious, but determined as ever to land the job. "I had to fly to New York and meet Jaffe so he could look me over and make the decision about whether I was good-looking enough. And that I wasn't still fat."

After two grueling auditions she was told she had the role. But Jaffe waited until a week before shooting began to give her a contract. "That was because they wanted to wait until the last minute to see if somebody better came along," says Jodie with more resignation than anger.

Loosely based on a vicious gang rape that took place in a New Bedford, Massachusetts, bar in the early eighties, *The Accused* is a harrowing tale of waitress Sarah Tobias's struggle to regain her dignity in the face of her unrepentant tormentors and a seemingly callous judicial system.

"I went straight into my emotions for that role. That was the catalyst. It was the juiciest role I've ever encountered," said Jodie.

Kaplan is a director with a reputation as a tough taskmaster, but Jodie reveled in his tough-love handling. "Jon Kaplan doesn't let you get away with anything," she said admiringly. "The minute I walked onto the set he yelled at me, 'Stop it, what are you doing with your hands? Do you have any idea how stupid that looks?' Actors are like kids, we do whatever we can get away with."

In subsequent movies that Jodie has directed or produced, she has taken her cues from Jon Kaplan, riding herd on the "kids" but trying not to be an "ogre."

The rape scene was shot over five grueling days on a closed set. Three strong sets of hands pinned her to the pinball machine, while the men simulated raping her over and over. Onlookers cheered the rapists on as though they were watching a sporting event, just as they had during the actual attack. When it was finished, a number of blood vessels in Jodie's eyes were broken from crying on cue so much.

Remembering the incident later, Jodie realized she had almost no memory of shooting it. "I blanked out. I was more emotionally involved than I've ever been before. I lived that experience in a way that I had never lived anything on screen. I'm not a bumbling, weepy woman obsessed with method acting, but never, not in my conscious memory, have I ever been so totally stripped of my will."

Sarah Tobias was a victim, but she was also one of Jodie's heroines because she refused to allow the rapists to get away with it. She is a flawed character with rough edges and a foul mouth, who has the provocative SXY SADIE for a vanity license tag. But in Jodie's rendering of the character, she finds an inner strength that elevates her, convincing a female prosecutor it is worth defying the odds to fight for justice. The performance was so convincing that Mom, certainly a consummate Hollywood pro who knows it's just make-believe, wept when she first saw the rape scene.

"Sarah is not exactly a mature, intelligent, sophisticated role model," says Jodie. "But she is human and is entitled to dignity and respect."

When the movie wrapped, Jodie was overcome with a feeling she had "failed miserably." She said, "I thought, when this movie comes out I'm really gonna be embarrassed." Resignedly she returned to Yale and took the graduate school entrance exams, intending vaguely to pursue a career as a writer or as an editor at a publishing company. "I was thinking, 'I'm not an actor. I was not meant to do this. I'm going to move to Nigeria and become a professor,' " she said.

At the time Mom's reaction was to breathe a sigh of relief. She had always preached that acting was a crap shoot. Jodie had already made a great deal of money. Mom's attitude was, spend your money getting a medical degree or law degree.

Our entire family agreed with Mom's assessment. During and after the Hinckley nightmare, being a relative of Jodie's was more than trying. With every new twist and turn in the plot, and the years of rehashing the story every time Jodie made a film or Hinckley gave an interview, reporters called our family and drove us crazy with impossible questions. It became an ordeal all of us wished would go away. So nobody in the family would have been sad if she had quit. Jodie's hope was that even if *The Accused* was her last hurrah, the movie would change some women's lives by giving them the strength to overcome the anguish of a sexual attack and would show men how devastating rape is for a woman.

The praise she received afterward was one of those moments that make life seem, as Jodie often says, predestined. Typical of the reviews was the *Los Angeles Times* rave: "It is an extraordinary performance." With a minor success she might well have gone ahead and quit the business. With an Academy Award she had no choice but to keep striving. She had become a mature leading lady.

Despite the huge turnaround the movie caused, the uncomfortable feeling remained that her performance was less than perfect. (At the time she actually said to Kaplan, "I'm sorry, I ruined your movie.") I've always noticed that as tough as Jodie is on others, and she can be very tough indeed, she is even more savage in her self-assessment. Looking back on all the movies prior to *The Accused*, she is merciless in her self-criticism. "I spent a lot of time acting like I thought everyone else on screen was an idiot. I always said acting wasn't stimulating enough, that it was beneath me in some way. But what I realized was that I was playing it safe, and it was up to me to make that extra leap.

"*The Accused* was the one moment in my life where I realized that what *I* wanted was to be an actor. That it was ultimately, completely, and totally satisfying."

Jodie's *Accused* Oscar speech was also a triumph. Unlike many actors who sputter drivel, Jodie succinctly expressed the reason the movie was made: "This is such a big deal, and my life is so simple. There are very few things—there's love, and work, and family. And this movie is so special to us because it was made for all three of those things. And I'd like to thank all of my families, the tribes that I come from, the wonderful crew on *The Accused* . . . and most importantly my mother, Brandy, who taught me that all my finger paintings were Picassos and that I didn't have to be afraid. And mostly that cruelty might be human, and it might be cultural, but it's not acceptable, which is what this movie is about. Thank you so much."

Whether she liked it or not, she was suddenly a major player in Hollywood, and to achieve her lifelong ambition to direct a film, she had only to ask. The downside as far as Jodie is concerned was that the thorny crown of fame grew heavier yet. As she has said with irony, "it's funny to be someone everyone has an opinion about."

Ironically, since she was riding the crest of her first Oscar win, her next picture was one Jodie says she is least proud of having made, Dennis Hopper's 1990 bomb *Backtrack*. If she wanted to "die for it" when she first said yes, she almost wanted Hopper to die after shooting began. At first the gangster-noir script sounded like great fun. Her character was a murder witness who falls in love with the hitman (Hopper) sent to rub her out. They go on the lam, fleeing both the mob and the FBI. Hopper's character is obsessed with Jodie: he carries a picture of her in a garter belt, an uncomfortable reference to Hinckley.

The shooting, in the New Mexico wilderness and at some of the locations used in Hopper's seminal sixties film *Easy Rider*, was an utter disaster, close to the worst she had experienced in more than twenty-five prior films. Uncharacteristically, Jodie agreed to a gratuitous nude shower scene, which she was assured would be strongly edited. Instead, just about every inch of footage was used, to the point that it was embarrassing, pointless, and voyeuristic. Naturally, she was furious when she saw the film, feeling betrayed, but it was too late. Prints had already been made and shipped, which of course seemed to have been deliberate.

"A week into the movie there was a side of me that had big question marks all over my forehead. Like, this is a joke, right? But if you ever ask Dennis how the experience went, he was as happy as a clam. He's clueless."

The film, which costarred everybody from Vincent Price to Bob Dylan, John Turturro to Joe Pesci, was finally released directly to video and cable. It was not what anyone would have expected of her after the triumph of *The Accused*. Luckily, she was already on her way to a new triumph.

TWELVE

There are a lot of conviction movies to be made, but I'd never work again if I made them. —JODIE FOSTER

The first time I ever heard Jodie mention the word *sequel* in a positive way was after she finished playing the role of Clarice Starling, the FBI trainee in *The Silence of the Lambs*. Like *The Accused*, *Silence* was a movie that spoke directly to the themes that had come to matter most to Jodie. And, like most of the roles Jodie considers to be important, she had to fight to get it and make it her own.

Jodie had actually been trying to buy the rights to Thomas Harris's novel for several years, and was beside herself when it was sold from under her. Despite the attention she had won with *The Accused*, she didn't have enough clout to compete for such a hotly contested prize against veteran producers. She received a double blow when she learned that Michelle Pfeiffer had been given the plum part.

Luckily, Pfeiffer turned down the offer after a money dispute.

Resolved that she would at least win the part back, Jodie flew to New York and met director Jonathan Demme. She explained that she had been psychologically working out the notion of victimization for years and wanted with all her heart to play the role of a hero cop who ends a reign of terror against women. She was displaying a combination of the confidence and determination that had carried her so far already.

Jodie felt that the Starling part was the first time in cinematic history when a genuine female hero wins out using female intuition and cleverness rather than brawn. Unlike characters such as Sigourney Weaver's Ripley in the *Alien* movies, or Linda Hamilton's character in *Terminator* 2, Starling is not a female macho figure. Yes, she has to use a gun in the final confrontation, but she is there only because she alone has been able to track the killer down. Her FBI superiors are all off on a wild-goose chase.

Throughout the film Starling demonstrates the superiority of her reasoning. Most obviously, she is able to piece together the clues to the killer's identity through careful, dispassionate analysis of what she observes. But in her dealings with the terrifying Hannibal Lecter, though she is forced to give up parts of her psychological self to satisfy him, she is able to get what she wants from him while he makes fools of others (mostly men). Just as Jodie made it through the chaos of our family by being removed from it, Starling is able to deal with the threats of Lecter and Buffalo Bill.

Of course, she expressed her reasons for being so

intently interested a little differently, but still the emphasis was on the polarity between men and women, between the physical and the mental. "Women didn't go to Vietnam and blow things up. They're not Rambo. I loathe the 'boys' movies' and would never do anything like that," Jodie said. "That's why *Silence of the Lambs* is such a big departure, because . . . you have a real female heroine. It's not about steroids and brawn; it's about using your mind . . . to combat the villain."

While at Yale, one of Jodie's favorite subjects was mythology. *Silence* struck her as a brilliant modern example of mythic adventure the minute she read it. The idea of the heroine having to go to a place of danger (Lecter's dungeon) from which she might never return in order to get the secret of how to slay the beast greatly excited her in its classic simplicity.

One of her favorite exchanges in the *Silence* script is when Agent Starling calmly but firmly chides her boss, Jack Crawford, played by Scott Glenn, for his blatantly sexist behavior toward her after the frightening autopsy scene. While driving away, Crawford tries to explain why she was excluded from an important discussion with local cops about grisly details of a murder.

JACK CRAWFORD

Starling, when I told that sheriff we shouldn't talk in front of a woman, it really burned you, didn't it? Well, that was just smoke.

CLARICE STARLING

It matters, Mr. Crawford. Cops look at you to see how you act. It matters.

To her relief, Jodie was soon on her way to track the fear-some killer on *Silence of the Lambs'* Pittsburgh set. But first she immersed herself in research, visiting the FBI's training school in Quantico, Virginia, and then a morgue to see how corpses are handled and autopsies performed.

Impressed with the agents who briefed her, Jodie said, "I admire these FBI guys a lot. I think they are genuine American heroes." She had a special sympathy in observing their real-life activities, which underscored how much more their work depended on the kind of mental activity Jodie respects than the shoot-'em-up stuff featured in most movies.

The FBI also provided a female special agent to show Jodie and Scott Glenn the grisly ropes of homicide work. Special Agent Mary Ann Kraus said, "Jodie was deeply affected by everything she saw, but she didn't flinch from any of it. We got out the photographs taken immediately after bodies are discovered, and Jodie saw it all, the bloated ones, the mutilated ones.

"We offered to play tapes made by two rapist-killers of the pleas and screams of their victims as they were tortured. Scott Glenn listened to them, but Jodie drew the line at that.

"She wasn't forced by anybody to see the things she saw, but she chose to and I admire her guts for that."

The Starling role, in an extremely well-written psycho-thriller, was the chance of a lifetime, and Jodie was deter-mined from the start to make it Oscar quality. As soon as filming began, director Demme knew he had made the right choice.

"It's the first character I can think of where Jodie didn't

have to hide the intelligence she possesses as a person," he said. "I think she's always had to mask that one way or another."

Anthony Hopkins also had the role of a lifetime as the brilliant, mad psychiatrist Dr. Hannibal Lecter, who has gone so far into the dark side he enjoys his murder victims braised and served with fava beans and a fine Chianti. "When I first read the part," Hopkins said, "I thought, 'This man is a cross between Truman Capote, Katharine Hepburn, and HAL, the computer in *2001*. A killing machine. Lecter is a personification of the devil, and I have always perceived the devil as very charming, witty, all clever and wise, seductive, sexual—and lethal.'"

The Lecter character sent a chill up the spine of even the FBI official charged with tracking serial killers. John Douglas, head of the bureau's Investigative Support Unit and a consultant on the film, said Lecter is "brilliant and completely evil, with incredible reflexes and an almost supernatural sense of smell. We've never come across anything like him—thank God."

The only thing more horrifying to the viewer than Lecter's deranged braggadocio is the sadistic delight his jailer takes in storing him in a dungeon and imprisoning his head in a bizarre, cruel, wire mask. The film has the audacity and wit to create a wounded yet proud monster, and make the audience squirm in their seats because it's so hard not to sympathize with him. In the end, when he escapes and boasts he is about to capture the jailer and have him for dinner, the viewers are almost glad for him.

The powerful relationship between Starling and Lecter is the psychological linchpin of the movie. Though both Jodie and Hopkins were already widely respected, their respective strengths and insights worked to the other's benefit in *Silence*. "I am able to play monsters well," Hopkins has said. "I understand madmen. I can understand what makes people tick in these darker levels." Pairing his understanding of evil with Jodie's passion for justice made for magic.

At the *Silence* Oscar celebration party, Jodie told me how much she was in awe of Hopkins's performance. "He was brilliant," she said, "and you've got to know him to appreciate how much. He's such a kind soul, so gentle, so very quiet. So *nice*. And for him to produce this creature of the sheerest evil, it's just an incredible achievement."

However, as is often the case, relations between Jodie and the film's director were less than perfect. Halfway through filming, Jodie strongly voiced her opinions of what Demme was doing wrong and how it could be fixed, in very specific, detailed terms. It was inevitable, really, that she would have her own strong ideas. She had been working on this project for years.

When he was told Jodie was trying to take over the film, Demme exploded. She recalled: "I had an opinion, and I said in my usual I-know-it-all voice, 'Well, I think you're in trouble. But there's a way to fix it: reshoot this, don't reshoot that, get rid of that person and hire somebody else.' Then I went home and never thought about it again.

"Monday morning the director takes me aside and says: 'I just want you to know one thing: This is *my* movie. You said we should do this and we should do that . . .'

"I said: 'I didn't say any such thing. Somebody asked my opinion, and I told them what it was.' "

After the angry exchange Jodie got "so flipped out" she

did a whole scene without the Southern accent she had perfected for the role of Agent Starling and "started mumbling and getting really mad." But in the end, when she had gotten to know Demme well, her view was completely different. "He really is the sweetest soul and such a good person. I almost didn't believe it at first. I thought he was full of shit, that he was manipulative because he's so nice! I thought no one is this nice. What's he trying to put over on me?"

Ironically, as prone to conflict as she was with Demme, Jodie's demeanor to others on the set was far more relaxed. As always she eschewed superstar treatment, and one morning on the set she gently corrected a continuity woman who was treating her a bit too reverently. "Mary, you can yell at me, call me an asshole—you don't have to tiptoe around."

In the end, Jodie's quest for a dream role and closure to her lifelong concern over victimization paid off. *Silence* won Oscars for Best Picture, Best Director, Best Actress, and Best Actor, as well as Best Screenplay.

Jodie hoped that the woman-as-hero idea would catch on in Hollywood and lead to twenty copycat films. *Silence* set a pretty good example by grossing more than $150 million. It was, Jodie felt, strong entertainment that was both popular and subtly struck a blow for womankind at the same time. It didn't happen immediately, but films like the recent *Copycat* and *Fargo* show that Hollywood is finally beginning to head in that direction.

Silence did have its dissenters, though. Jodie simply could not understand them. *Mademoiselle*'s critic blasted the film, claiming it was pornographic and exploitative, charges that infuriated Jodie. "We took great pains to keep it from being exploitative. It was the same way with *The Accused*. People said, 'Why do you have to show the rape?' If we hadn't had it in the movie, the movie wouldn't have said what it was supposed to say.

"You can't make a movie like *Silence*, which ultimately deals with the pain and horror of death, and not have death in front of your eyes. Violence is a part of life for men and women."

When one interviewer asked what she says to people who complain her movies are too violent toward women, Jodie said, "I hit them with my Oscar."

The *Silence* triumph brought changes in power, prestige, and money, but I also think the movie, and the depth to which Jodie immersed herself in the Starling role, served to provide a catharsis that is immeasurably important to my sister. Since *Silence* Jodie has acted in three movies directed by others, and directed three more, and is, at this writing, working on a fourth. In none of them is she a victim. None of them are about victims. The movies in which Jodie has been the guiding force are instead all about making connections in some way or another.

The directing efforts since then have all touched on issues such as innocence and precociousness and isolation (*Little Man Tate* and *Nell*) as well as a more mature resignation that conflict is an inevitable part of intimacy (*Home for the Holidays*).

Still, the major concern I have long felt about Jodie was not the tabloid's frenzy over what kind of lovers she had, but her lack of any kind of intimate relationship with anybody. She is a very hard person to be intimate with; Jodie has always felt a great need to keep a shield between her and the world. The notion that intimacy is dangerous was pounded into her by Mom from the time she was old enough to talk. Mom demonstrated her inner agony on a regular basis and stressed our father was at fault.

Experiences like the Hinckley episode reinforced Jodie's guardedness. It often seems Jodie's goal is to be an impartial observer of life, to be a character in an endless, seamless play rather than a participant who has to deal with the messy and sometimes hurtful parts of love and life. I know that I have spent far too much time and emotion coupling and uncoupling, but it strikes me as somehow sad that a beautiful, rich, intelligent, and charming young woman has no one to share her life with.

When we were growing up there were always fights over the bathroom and the quarters were always cramped, which led Jodie to say frequently she couldn't stand the idea of voluntarily sharing a bathroom with anyone again. But I am surprised that she has kept her vow this long.

"I am a loner, a solitary person," Jodie says. "I like to spend the day alone, I enjoy eating alone. That's why I like Paris, you are alone but with others. But I'm not lonely and I never have been."

Mom has also led a solitary life since Jodie moved out. Jodie is following Mom's script in her personal life as she once did in her professional life. I hope she doesn't wake up one morning and, like Katharine Hepburn, wish she had cared less for her art and more for herself, wishing futilely she had children and grandchildren.

I was not surprised that Jodie said recently one of the most significant moments in her life came during the filming of a scene in the movie *Nell*. As brilliant as she is, I can't imagine that if she had stopped to think about that comment she wouldn't appreciate the irony of it. *Nell*, after all, is just a movie; the question was about her real life. But since she was a toddler, movies have been her life.

Mom has been the major influence in Jodie's life up until now, and frankly, she has molded her into a work robot. Eighteen-hour days are common for her when shooting a film, and usually one film follows another, with little or no break, working from conception, to script, casting, preproduction, shooting, and editing right through the publicity campaign.

Jodie has spent almost her entire life working for applause, and I doubt she will ever be able to stop. She said recently, "When I was a little kid, the director would say, 'I would like you to put your toe on this left corner and twirl your head at a certain angle and do this.' My whole point in life was to follow to the most minute detail absolutely everything they wanted me to be. And when I accomplished that I got a lot of applause."

Interestingly, some of the highest compliments people in the business pay Jodie have to do with her workaholic habits; bizarrely, the word most often used to describe her is *machine*.

Sommersby director John Amiel said, "If God had designed a perfect acting machine it would be pretty close to Jodie." *Little Man Tate* producer Scott Rudin, with whom she repeatedly clashed over the film's direction, admiringly called her "an extremely well-oiled machine."

Admittedly, the dysfunctionality of our early life, the lack of a father, the terror that our troubled mother was going to desert us as well, are negatives that Jodie has turned into positives.

The psychologist John Bradshaw, whom I credit along with George Blair with turning my life around, drew a paradigm that I think fits Jodie perfectly. He said that many of the most successful people come from difficult, challenging backgrounds. They climb a mountain, and then they immediately look for another to climb. The journey must be increasingly difficult, the road steeper and steeper, to satisfy the hunger inside.

Jodie thinks she takes time off from work, but she really doesn't, especially considering how hard she works. Most actors try to get completely away from Hollywood and work for extended periods between projects to relax and recharge their batteries. I've never seen Jodie have much time to herself. One thing she does to relax is drive out into the desert and take long, solitary walks. She says it is a time to meditate, to make decisions, and to recharge from the tensions and stress she is always under.

She virtually has no home. There is a house in the far San Fernando Valley, nearly an hour from town, which she has owned for six years. But she has never really lived in it, never entertained in it, and it was put up for sale in November 1995. The house was something she bought on a whim, because it seemed as though a millionaire should at least own a house. And on a day of bad smog and traffic, she felt she needed to get away from Los Angeles because it's so "scuzzy." But the house was too far out in the valley. It's a totally impractical location for someone who needs to be at studios and in Hollywood all the time. So now she rents a guest house—the fourth in the last couple of years—deliberately avoiding a sense of permanency or roots.

Jodie's attitude toward her house is very revealing. She likes to say that your car shows what you would like people to think you are like, and your house shows what you are really like. Her car is eminently practical, safe, black, and opaque. But her house is filled with antiques, rare books, and art, including one of her more curious selections, a Eugene Jardin sculpture of an African beast menacing a naked woman, which is set in the middle of the sparsely furnished living room.

The Valley house was built in 1934 as the guest house of a country estate owned by Hungarian director Michael Curtiz, who directed *Casablanca* in 1942. The home is surrounded by a high wall on about half an acre. Jodie completely remodeled it, adding imported glass mosaic tiles from Italy to the master bathroom and twenty-two-karat gold leaf detailing on the ceiling in the master bedroom. The redesign was done by our sister Connie. Curiously, Jodie rhapsodizes about it, but only in the abstract. She said recently, "It's so beautiful and so personalized and every detail is so unique and old, with old books and beautiful stained glass that was there in the twenties, and a rotunda and all this land, which is all trees and not landscaped." Or most of it, anyway.

She pays great attention to her beautiful garden, often working on it herself.

Jodie has been collecting arty black-and-white photographs and first editions of French literature for years and has an impressive collection in the house. By far her favorite photograph is of the swollen hands of an elderly grape picker, taken in Eastern Europe in the forties. It's a symbol of the cost of a lifetime of hard work.

Jodie gets very dramatic when she talks about her frugality and her abhorrence of Hollywood extravagance: "I'd rather die than have thirty paintings in my house that are all worth $7 million. So what I have are some cheap but beautiful photographs."

All the same, Jodie says she gets "really depressed" if she stays in her house for more than a day. She yearns to get back to the rented place, where there is absolutely nothing that belongs to her.

Jodie has a hard time with the concept of acquiring material things. She *complains* that people constantly give her expensive clothes and other items. When she looks in her closets and finds them stuffed full of clothes she doesn't have any recollection of buying, it is unsettling. The solution is to use a friend's garage for a giant sale. When it is done and all the designer clothes, souvenirs, and other gifts are gone, she can breathe a sigh of relief and get on with her life, unburdened.

Even her car, which is extremely modest in a town where $200,000 Rolls-Royces and turbo Bentleys are commonplace, made her uncomfortable until its patina was tarnished. "My car drives me crazy. When I first got it I was so upset all the time worrying about it. But once I got a few dings in it, I was okay."

Right now Jodie declares her "life is on hold," but sometime in the future she will shop for a new home closer to Hollywood. Until then, having people visit at her house is out of the question. "I don't like people coming to my house, obviously," she says. "I don't have things delivered. I don't let *them* know where I live."

The obvious answer is that Jodie needs someone to share her house with, but a suggestion like that would get her blood boiling. She is unapologetically contemptuous toward the idea that people need family for fulfillment. "There is nothing that annoys me more than all of my friends who are over forty who desperately want to have children by fifty because basically they want someone to love them," Jodie says. "It's too desperate. If I have kids, I have them. If I don't, I don't."

Jodie's mostly solitary life works for her. She could be surrounded by an army of people if she wanted, but that would make her miserable. She is introspective, unapologetically eccentric, and very much enjoys her own company.

Jodie's independence in recent years has been hard for Mom to take. For most of the years of her career, Jodie never gave an interview without Mom being present. Mom would answer the questions for her, sometimes even contradicting Jodie's responses. The two were often photographed together, Mom looking at her daughter with loving admiration, like the woman behind the throne. But in the past few years Mom and Jodie have drifted apart. There was no one dramatic incident between them, but little by little Jodie has broken away. Mom is no longer invited to the interviews, and reporters are specifically told not to contact Brandy Foster for her perspective on Jodie's latest film.

It's a remarkable change in a complex relationship between the two women. Just a few years ago Jodie was talking about her need for Mom's presence when she went overseas to work on a film, as though she were a fainthearted little girl: "I need someone familial for the first couple of weeks, because I not only get lonely but disoriented." She bragged about their ability to tell each other to shut up, when one or the other gets in a bad mood, without permanently hurt feelings. The confrontations between them that I have seen in recent years have gotten far more hard-edged and hurtful.

"I do have a strange relationship with her," Jodie has admitted. "When you are a single parent, it has edges and mixed messages that other people don't have. It's more intimate and it gets uglier. She pisses me off. We yell at each other."

When interviews get personal, Jodie sometimes seems to say more than she intends to, but her suggestion that Mom has been often less than honest with us rings true to me. "Women's relationships with their mothers are very complicated anyway," Jodie told a *Los Angeles Times* reporter a few years ago. "When you have that [intimate] relationship with your child, you can show them the ugliest parts about you, your child can't leave, can't abandon you.

"My feeling is that children can take any piece of information you can give them, but they can't take being lied to. You can say, 'Look, I've been in jail,' and they can handle it because . . . kids are very resilient that way. It's the stuff that's hidden that's most abusive.

"Look, my mom is just more interested in her children's lives than in her own. We've always had a very hermetic life. It wasn't about other people. It was closed and very intense behind those four walls."

In the late eighties a writer brought Jodie a book called *The*

Drama of the Gifted Child by Alice Miller, a psychological analysis of the interaction between extremely bright children and their parents. Later Jodie said she resented having the book thrust at her, viewing it as an uninvited intrusion, but she did admit that Miller's evaluation was eerily close to the mark.

Miller wrote that gifted children learn and practice behavior that will get maximum love and approval from their parents. The more positive reinforcement, or applause, they get, the greater the effort will be to manipulate. What they lose in the bargain is their own sense of identity. But they tend to get better and better at pleasing their parent and eventually take over the parental role, even taking over the responsibility for their siblings.

Curiously, around the same time Adrian Lyne, who directed *Foxes*, commented on the relationship between Mom and Jodie, saying it was hard to tell who the parent was: "It was strange. You felt that Jodie was more mature than her mother."

At family get-togethers Jodie displays her ascendant role as well. At a dinner not long ago, Mom attacked me, dredging up my failed marriages and how she had told me so, for the umpteenth time. This was ground I definitely didn't want to go over again in front of the family and my wife Stacy. I was embarrassed to have to deal with it in front of everybody, but she was relentless.

To my surprise, Jodie exploded at her: "How dare you, Mother! You have no right to talk to him like that, to treat your son that way."

Mom looked as though she had been smacked in the face. An icy silence descended, and the two women steeled their faces and eyed each other warily. It reminded me of Grandma Lucy's castigation of Mom back when we were children and she pushed Jodie into her room.

After dinner, when we were all leaving, Jodie came to me and put her arm on my shoulder. "She'll never change, Bud, so don't even wish for that. But she does love you."

For herself, Jodie says she does her best to ignore the sometimes withering criticism she gets from Mom over whatever film or personal project she is involved in. "It's just in one ear and out the other," she says.

Like most artists, Jodie deals with her inner turmoil through her art. In fact, she says she considers acting and moviemaking therapy. But Jodie will never allow in an interview that her art imitates her family life sometimes.

However, the films, like *Little Man Tate* and *Holidays*, that Jodie completely controls are a mirror on her soul. It's a fact she won't freely acknowledge, but she does pay grudging respect to critics and observers who see the deeply, sometimes painfully personal strain that runs through her oeuvre.

Jodie has always said therapy is one of the best forms of education, and her films are her means of introspection and self-analysis. Though she strongly supports therapy for others, she has never turned to it for help with her own problems. The mere thought of Jodie pouring out her heart to a therapist is laughable. I doubt she would be capable of doing it even if she wanted to. Some inner fuse would pop, rendering her temporarily mute. Her solution to emotional turmoil is to plunge into work and lose herself in it. Acting is what eases her pain.

THIRTEEN

*I'd like to explore female sexuality in a way
that people don't get to see on screen.*
                                    —JODIE FOSTER

*S*ilence would change Jodie's career forever. But first it
started a protracted legal war with Orion Pictures. On
the night that she won her Oscar, Jodie had already
been worrying, with Mom's help, about Orion's financial
condition. The Oscar sweep meant a windfall for the
studio's coffers, much of which they owed Jodie. But the fortune *Silence* was making disappeared down a black hole of
creative accounting in an attempt to make up for other,
failed projects.

Orion soon declared bankruptcy and refused to pay the
money earned by Jodie and the other stars who had essen-
tially built the production company. When the payments
for *Silence* were abruptly halted, Jodie was deeply into *Little
Man Tate,* her directorial debut, which unfortunately was
also financed by Orion Pictures. She had no choice but to

fight two separate battles against the studio, one to get the money she was owed for her last film and the other to keep *Tate* from going down the tubes.

A bitter and exhausting legal fight was finally won. Jodie emerged victorious but disgusted with the Hollywood way of doing business. Vowing never again to fall victim to the greed and mendacity that typifies Hollywood, she turned down extremely lucrative offers from every major and minor studio in town for so-called independent production deals. It was a gutsy move that had most of her advisers reeling. Instead she signed a $100 million deal with PolyGram Records' new division, PolyGram Filmed Entertainment, because it wasn't a studio and had no plans to become one.

The deal she eventually cut with PolyGram was nothing short of incredible. It financed six pictures over three years, three in the $25-million range and three in the $10- to $15-million range, plus $10 million per film for publicity and prints. Jodie would have sole power to decide which movies to make and whether to produce, direct, star, do all three, or none. And she was given complete control over every aspect of the films, creatively as well as financially. It is a unique business arrangement in the annals of Hollywood, particularly considering her age. With that fortune behind her, she formed Egg Pictures and, just thirty years old, was CEO of her own multimillion dollar Hollywood production company.

The reason she was able to secure such a contract is, of course, because she has proven box office clout. Jodie Foster is one of three or four women (Demi Moore, Julia Roberts, Sharon Stone, and maybe Meg Ryan) who can "open" a movie, that is, guarantee that on the critical first weekend of release, particularly a big holiday weekend, theaters will be packed just because of the name on the marquee. Jodie has also shown solid judgment in picking projects and sound fiscal sense in making them. But there are others that have those qualities. The key is her history, over a period of thirteen years, of always showing up on time, never going back on her word, and being able to keep a secret; it was, in large measure, a tribute to her character.

As stern as Jodie is about ethics, she is generally nonjudgmental toward others because she recognizes her position is somewhat unique. Unlike most people, she has a product—herself—that is so good she can ram it down people's throats. She has no need to cut corners, exaggerate, or jiggle the truth. Few people have that luxury. With far less than the freight train load of cash in the bank Egg Pictures received, many fledgling production companies have gone berserk with Lear jets, yachts, and grotesquely bloated movie budgets. The bean counters at PolyGram, who gave Jodie virtual carte blanche, would have smiled had they sat in on a meeting soon after the deal was signed. In it Jodie sternly lectured her executives that the modest furniture expenditures for their new office must not go a nickel over budget.

The offices are tasteful but frugally decorated, especially compared to those of other titans. In the center of her office is a large pine desk; oriental rugs that are nice, but not antique or hand woven, are scattered about, and a life-size Hannibal Lecter cutout leers menacingly. No Oscars or other awards are in sight; they are at Mom's house in the "Jodie shrine" room. In addition to the black-and-white photos on the walls, some of which are of the family and were taken by Jodie, there is a framed poster from a

Minneapolis film festival that honored her and a *Little Man
Tate* poster.

Scattered about the office are dog-eared books, mostly in
French, on art and poetry (mostly Baudelaire), and copies of
Paris Match magazine. On the desk and coffee table are
lucky charms that were given to her at critical points in her
career. The talismans include a magic eight ball, a stuffed
pig, and a black plastic dragon.

All in all, Jodie's Egg Pictures offices are more like a college professor's office than a movie mogul's. They have a
personal touch, but she doesn't want her office to feel too
much like home. "I don't keep anything important here. If I
were totally invested in it, then the office would be my
house, not where I work."

Even before she was ensconced in the Egg offices, Jodie
was displaying her drive and professionalism. During the
making of *Little Man Tate* she kept up a killing pace,
working eighteen-hour days for nearly seven months. Even
over Thanksgiving and Christmas she was on the job, fret-
ting over every detail, demanding perfection of herself and
everyone involved in the project. The strain during the difficult two-and-a-half-year filming of *Tate*, combined with the
court fray, took a toll that included slipping back into
smoking cigarettes, a habit she had kicked years before.

Adding to her problems was a running battle with producer Scott Rudin, who wanted to keep a tight rein on her
first directorial effort. Their struggle turned into the nastiest
she has ever had in Hollywood. She felt Rudin's presence on
the set was a direct challenge to her authority as director.
The result was a true battle of wills. Their arguments were
blazing rows. The degree of rancor got so bad, Jodie decided

she was not going to kiss and make up no matter what. Even sometime later Rudin's repeated attempts to mend fences with her fell on deaf ears. As an olive branch he even offered her another movie to direct. She rejected it out of hand.

Her stinging attacks on Rudin during the *Tate* publicity campaign were uncharacteristically vitriolic. I know Jodie thinks many of the people in the business are odious, but she has rarely engaged in public mudslinging. I have never heard her attack anyone with the bitterness she displayed toward Rudin. She told *Vanity Fair*, Rudin is "the person that exemplifies everything that's negative and everything that's a cliché about Hollywood. For him it's just about acquiring elements. I am a filmmaker."

She has had a powerful temper since she was a toddler. But Jodie's bluster is most often a cover for a deep vulnerability, a sensitive soul, as she puts it. Jodie has often told the story of how she once almost quit acting after a run-in with a particularly dictatorial director. "I never considered myself vulnerable to any kind of psychological insult. And I got on this set, and for some reason this director insulted my soul and it really took me a long time after that to be able to work again with confidence." Yet as often as she has told that story, she has never identified the director involved. Jodie doesn't like to take her feuds public. The fact that she blasted Rudin shows how truly furious she was.

Life at the top was going to get harder. After a love fest that lasted about two years, Jodie and PolyGram clashed and wound up in court. The falling-out shocked many in Hollywood, who were convinced the marriage was made in heaven. During the summer of 1996 Jodie was unceremoniously dumped from the psychological thriller *The Game* in which she was to costar with Michael Douglas. Her $54.5 million lawsuit claimed she had an oral agreement with PolyGram and Propaganda Films to do four weeks' work on the movie and had taken herself "off the market" for the summer in good faith. Not only that, they had used her name to raise money for the project, knowing all the while they had no intention of actually using her or paying the promised $4.5 million fee plus five percent of the gross. Further stirring the pot was Michael Douglas's muscle flexing. He claimed he had script approval, meaning he could change Jodie's lines without her consent and she would be forced to play her character anyway *he* wanted her to. Needless to say, that was a condition she would never agree to accept. To add insult to injury, according to Jodie, the producers spread nasty rumors that she was being so difficult on the set they had to get rid of her.

Suddenly the dream relationship was looking very sour and would drag through the courts. But, as is typical in Hollywood, she was still in bed with PolyGram, since her deal was still in place and in fact had just been renewed for an additional three years. There was clearly going to be some squirming beneath the sheets.

Sitting in the director's chair for the first time on the set of *Little Man Tate* back in 1991, Jodie found herself in charge of a small army and a $10 million budget. At age twenty-nine it was a heady experience, despite the fact she had been prepping for it since age eight. And it brought out the "bossy little thing" syndrome like nothing else ever had.

"Sometimes I say to myself, 'I'm not going to be bossy this time,'" Jodie recalled. "And I step back and stay in my trailer. But when you are emotionally involved in a movie, you want it to be good. Yeah, I'm pretty bossy. And as a director it's not any different than what I do as an actress, except that I'm allowed to."

Tate was a project that she cared very much about. The story of a seven-year-old whiz-kid's inner turmoil struck a chord with her. Jodie saw Fred Tate as "a misfit who is handicapped by exception."

Her inspiration for wanting to make the film was the J. D. Salinger novella *Franny and Zooey*, a lesser-known work than *Catcher In the Rye* but equally resonant in the early fifties when it was written, and popular with college students ever since. The book changed her life, she says, making her see relationships in a wholly different way.

Franny and Zooey is the story of two supersensitive genius siblings and their interior and exterior strivings. Jodie read the story, and all of Salinger's relative handful of works, when she was a teenager and has been haunted by Seymour Glass and the other characters ever since.

Additionally *Tate* is the tale of a tough, sometimes vulgar, single mother struggling to raise her son on a very tight budget. Jodie plays her character Dede as an edgy, defensive woman who seems equal part rage and love, much like our mother. It was hard for me to watch the film and not see it as a bittersweet homage to her own childhood.

"I show something I've never before chosen to show on screen, a totally warm, totally loving woman," said Jodie. "I've built most of my characters on strength."

The role of Fred Tate was difficult to cast. Jodie didn't want a child actor to *play* the quirky character; she wanted to find someone who *was* him. The search took her to dozens of Southern California schools to interview hundreds of potential children. When Adam Hann-Byrd, with his long, blond, braided ponytail, walked into the audition room, she knew she had found the boy for the job. He was painfully shy, answered questions with one-word answers, and focused on reading the part to the exclusion of all else. He clearly possessed the personality of a young whiz kid, struggling to master his gift and have a decent childhood at the same time. And he had the "lonely, sad, thoughtful" personality she wanted to portray. Over a period of months Jodie played with Adam day after day, teaching him judo and getting him to gradually trust her and to allow her to hug and kiss him, as she would have to do repeatedly, playing his mother in the film.

Cast to play Hann-Byrd's male mentor figure was singer/pianist Harry Connick, Jr., himself a musical prodigy. Jodie was fascinated watching the male bonding ritual between them. "When I saw how Harry was with Adam, how Adam laughed hysterically, then you know that it doesn't matter how much you feed him, clothe him, and take care of him, they want to be with some guy. They want their dad or their brother—they want some male figure. Adam was totally in love with Harry."

Jodie says she can't relate to wanting a male figure around, never having really known our father. Instead, she fondly recalls the sisterly relationship she had with Mom and the complex nature of their bond; Mom as friend, disciplinarian, and guru, Jodie as daughter, sister, pal, and husband substitute.

Jodie summed up her vision succinctly when *Tate* was released, saying, "There's the single-parent theme. And there's the theme that runs through all of my work, which is that I tend to deal with mundane heroes. Not people who build bridges, but people who are moral survivors in a world that's really cruel."

Initially Jodie didn't want to act in the film. But Orion demanded that she have a lead role. In the end, either Jodie acted in the movie or they would withdraw financing. The choice was tough for her because she believes acting and directing "for me, anyway, just don't go together at all."

Most of the executives hired by Jodie to work on *Tate* were women, as were the crew members and technical people, something she says she didn't "consciously" do. But it clearly suited her. She said, "The atmosphere on *Tate* was so good . . . it was like a real world, not just a film world where it's guys, guys, guys—macho madness."

Critics gave high marks for her directing and acting, though *Daily Variety* noted, "Most of the film's emotional power lies in the open, alert, eager-to-please face of Hann-Byrd (Fred Tate). Filled with small, telling moments rather than big events, the film never really gets inside Fred's head." I suspect the reason is that letting the viewer inside Fred's head would mean exposing the inside of Jodie's head. Other critics praised her "graceful visual style and assured touch with actors."

Shortly after the film was released, Jodie was devastated, overhearing two strangers slamming the movie. "I was on the back of a bus and heard someone say the film is just about two women, one of them is smart and one is stupid. The other said, 'How can you watch that?' I think I died a little bit."

She was aware *Tate* was a movie that defied categorization. It certainly wasn't an action adventure, a date movie, or "based on a Stephen King novel," and she wasn't going to compromise and let Orion sell it that way. Instead she went for a fairly unique promotion strategy, stimulating interest at the grassroots level by showing it at high schools, to Planned Parenthood groups, and giving endless interviews to special-interest magazines and local newspapers. Although the publicity drive was exhausting, it proved that there was a niche for a little movie "about misfits."

Tate was typical of Jodie's sense of proportion and economy. The film cost about $10 million, which is modest at a time when movies typically cost from $20 million up to the stratospheric $150 million Kevin Costner reportedly spent on *Waterworld*. Tate eventually grossed about $25 million domestically, but reached over $50 million with international sales, cable, and video cassettes.

Jodie savored her first directing job. "I love moviemaking because you have a hundred twenty people working together. If you can get them to believe they're part of the end product, you can get them to live up to the potential they could never have otherwise."

As savvy as she is about the mechanics of filmmaking, though, the actual task was far trickier than she had imagined. "I originally thought the director has this vision, this train that everybody puts their bags on. But now I realize the train has a life of its own."

Self-critical as always, Jodie gave her first directorial effort a mixed review at best. "There's one reel I still can't watch."

Soon afterward she packed her bags again and flew to New York for a cameo in a Woody Allen film. The legendary director-actor is one of the major inspirations for Jodie's personal style of filmmaking. His eccentric, quirky tales, in which he often seems to be having a private dialogue with the camera about the most private aspects of his life, have always appealed to Jodie. The thought of her actually making a movie in which she revealed her neuroses, sexual hang-ups, etcetera, is so out of the question for Jodie as to be almost laughable. But in her far more subtle and indirect way, she has expressed equally intimate longings, fears, and desires.

After hoping to work with Allen for years, Jodie finally got her chance in 1992 when she was able to take a small role in his film *Shadows and Fog*. It was a perfect film for Jodie to be associated with and a great chance to watch Allen in action. The movie was as arty and purposeful as anything he has made. Shot in "exquisite" black-and-white, it was described by *Daily Variety* as "a sweet homage to German expressionist filmmaking and a nod to the content of socially responsible tales." The movie is richly layered with bizarre sets and surreal characters. Jodie's scene takes place in a whorehouse where the "just visiting" Mia Farrow is badgered into selling herself just once. There is a traveling circus that is menaced by a strangler, gangs of marauding vigilantes, a cameo by Madonna as the adulterous wife of the circus strongman, and great doses of dark, menacing shadow and thick fog.

Appearing only briefly, lounging in the brothel and talking about the universe, Jodie seemed relaxed and thrilled to lie back and watch Allen's action swirl around her. Though expecting to see an original and eccentric director at work, Jodie was startled by just how strange Allen's style turned out to be.

"Nobody reads the script, nobody knows what the movie is about or what your character is about. They don't tell you where you're going to be or what time period it is. Basically, it's his movie—it's in his head."

Nevertheless, Jodie compares Allen to Martin Scorsese, whom she considers the best living American director, saying "each film evolves their character and the things they believe in," something she is striving to duplicate in her own work. She doesn't attempt to hide her scorn for directors who jump at whatever commercial job that happens to come along, with no concern for the underlying truth of the work.

Her next movie, *Sommersby*, was Jodie's first attempt at playing a romantic leading lady. The role called for soft backlighting, heavy-duty makeup sessions, and lots of love scenes with costar Richard Gere.

"It was a gamble," said producer Steven Reuther. "There were the obvious romantic leading females, and she wasn't one of them. Also, I don't think anybody had ever seen Jodie in a period costume. But once we got her in the period clothes and the hair, it was like, 'How could there ever have been a question?'"

Based loosely on the French film *The Return of Martin Guerre*, the Reconstruction–era film was shot in rural Virginia. In the story, a Confederate officer, thought long dead, returns to his wife after seven years a changed man. He turns out to be an imposter, but by the time he is found out, the wife, Laurel Sommersby, decides he is far better than the real husband and decides to keep him anyway. Fate intervenes as he is charged with murder and, ironically, tried by a black judge.

The key to the film is whether or not Jodie's Laurel Sommersby and her entire village really believe that her returning husband has changed from an abusive oaf into a loving, considerate husband, or if they are just going along with his charade. Grounded in reality as ever, Jodie believed her character is fully aware the man is not her husband but chooses to accept him because she needs a man and he appears to be a good one. Jodie thought Laurel's motivation is partly psychosexual as well; the element of danger in having this imposter in her bed fulfills her secret fantasy of a sexy, unpredictable stranger. The reason the townspeople go along is because they feel sorry for her having to survive on her own with a child for so many years, and pretend she isn't having a sinful relationship with a handsome stranger.

Richard Gere, who had painstakingly brought the project to fruition over a period of years, preferred to see the character's motivation the opposite way, believing he is a fraud but a successful one.

When Jodie first read the script, she was appalled at how weepy and wimpy the Laurel Sommersby character is and insisted that it be rewritten. In order for her to take the part Laurel had to be made into a lusty, frontier-type woman who wanted Gere's character for passion, not to be protected. What did appeal to her were the elements of a single mother surviving on her own, and men who are both other than what they seem and less than reliable. Sommersby was even a military officer, just like Dad.

Jodie invited my wife and me to watch the first screening at the Directors Guild building in West Hollywood. When we arrived she was across the room surrounded, as usual at events like that, by a gaggle of friends and admirers, so we merely waved. But she fought her way through the crowd, which was a daunting task considering nearly everyone she passed struggled to get her attention.

The reason for the urgency was to say in her most enigmatic and conspiratorial tone that I would be able to strongly identify with Gere's character.

Naturally, I watched the movie with rapt interest, wondering when the resemblance to my life would strike me. It never did, and to this day I am confused by what she meant. The only similarity I could see was that I had left my family to fight my own version of a war and had returned to an ambivalent reception at best. But it shows the extent to which she sees real-life people and problems in all her films.

Jodie, who had never worked with Gere before, was amused at the way young women swooned in his presence. "I don't get it at all, why anybody would squeal over Richard. He's very image-conscious, whether he admits it or not. He wears black pants every day, and he's got the same leather jacket every day. It's a guy thing. He needs to be cool." Still, he clearly fascinated Jodie, particularly when contrasted with her later *Maverick* costar and friend Mel Gibson. "Richard feels very dangerous, like a spiderweb you could get stuck in. Mel's just a kid."

Sommersby's budget was gigantic, nearly in the epic range, featuring platoons of cavalry, hundreds of extras, and truckloads of period costumes. This army was under the command of British director Jon Amiel, who had never directed a movie with a budget over $5 million and was best known for thrifty BBC-TV work.

Amiel and Jodie, who at the time had made over thirty films, clashed repeatedly. She later admitted wryly, "I definitely had lots of opinions about how the movie was run. It was nice for him to know there was someone else watching out for him." Actually, Jodie was furious with Amiel for much of the time the massive company was on location in the Virginia wilderness. She felt very unfairly treated by the young director compared with Richard Gere, whom Amiel seemed to respect, or fear, more.

"Directors do this with actresses. They like to watch them jump through hoops. He'd make me do six setups and fifty takes for no good reason. I'm good on the first take. I know this about me. But he thought it was fun. You look at the rushes, and there are endless takes on Jodie and one on Richard, because he's the guy."

Despite the friction with Amiel, Jodie got on famously with the often mercurial Gere. Toward the end of the shoot, when she admired Gere's wife Cindy Crawford's necklace, the actor ordered an identical one for Jodie, which he presented with a flourish during a taped interview they gave. Gere said the chemistry between them was as good as he'd had with Julia Roberts in *Pretty Woman*, which was the biggest hit of his career.

Unfortunately, despite the star power of Gere and Jodie, *Sommersby* opened big but had wobbly legs. It paid for itself, but failed to become the certified hit Gere and the producers expected. Fortunately, Jodie was already on the way to another success.

The 1994 cowboy farce *Maverick* with James Garner, with whom she had last worked as a ten-year-old on *One Little*

Indian, and Mel Gibson was one of the happiest experiences of her career and added a comedic dimension to her acting repertoire. It was also a genuine smash hit.

Jodie was again hired only after another actress unexpectedly dropped out. This time Meg Ryan quit the project, and anxious producers were forced to scramble to keep the film on schedule. Jodie had two days to read the script, make a decision, and show up on the set. The last comedic role she had taken was the Disney comedy *Candleshoe,* seemingly a lifetime before, in 1977. For ten years Jodie had been vainly searching for a good comedy, though she was slightly nervous about keeping up with Garner, notorious for his ad-libbing.

Once the shooting started, though, the ad-libbing, joking, and pratfalls came naturally. The three actors had so much fun ad-libbing, they wondered if the movie was going to make any sense. Certainly part of Jodie's enthusiasm for the role had come from the fact that the William Goldman script was brilliant. The author of *Butch Cassidy and the Sundance Kid* and *The Sting* proved he still had the flare. Goldman might have had a little trouble recognizing his script, but he had given three terrific actors great material to work with.

Jodie not only kept up with the boys but created a memorable character in the mold of classic sassy Western heroines, although one distinctly her own. She played the vampish, almost slapstick role for all it was worth, nearly going over the top at some points. It was a major coup, convincing critics who normally hate actors trying to stretch that the casting was "inspired."

Jodie had no game plan when the cameras rolled, and she

discovered Gibson and Garner had given no particular thought to it either. On one of the first days of shooting Jodie, wearing an enormous period dress, was perched precariously at the door of a stagecoach, hoping someone was going to help her down. Instead she slipped and belly flopped, facedown on the ground. The cameras kept rolling, and Jodie went with it, beginning her first ad-libbing of the movie. From that moment the Annabelle Bransford character was played with a zany clumsiness that was in perfect juxtaposition to the formal clothes.

Jodie managed to strike a blow for feminism as well. Her lusty (mostly for money) Annabelle Bransford manages to shoot a gun at the bad guys, something traditional women in Westerns were discouraged from doing. And she pulls a clever, successful con game on men, another no-no in traditional films of the genre. But most important, Annabelle survives on her own terms, even in the rough and tumble "man's world" of the Old West. She is not tied to the railroad tracks and is not rescued and carried away dangling over the star's broad shoulder.

The premiere gala for *Maverick* was held at a Westwood restaurant that was completely decorated in Old West style for the night. The high-spirited fun of the shoot was apparent at the celebration. The cast and crew all knew by then that they had made a rollicking good comedy, which was a surefire box office hit.

An additional benefit of *Maverick* was the friendship that arose between Mel Gibson and Jodie. When the film was in the can, they went on a camping trip in Bryce Canyon, Utah. At the premiere party Jodie bubbled over with enthusiasm for her new friend and the trip they shared. "It was fantastic,

Buddy," she gushed. "We went backpacking into the wilderness, camped out, went all over the park."

It's interesting to speculate, now that Gibson has won a Best Director Oscar, what another film pairing of the immensely talented duo would be like. But I doubt that kind of hookup was much on Jodie's mind at the time. She was ready to return to directing again, and with a tour de force that would be another sign of her distinctive vision.

FOURTEEN

I'm not interested in facts. I'm interested in truth, which is different.
　　　　　　　　　—JODIE FOSTER

Jodie makes a clear philosophical distinction between the films she directs and the films in which she acts. The acting jobs are attempts to bring to life situations and people she has never experienced and likely never will. The films she directs are "personal essays," lessons in how she thinks people should deal with reality and their own souls. At least that's how she thinks of them when she starts working. She has been surprised by the fact that the films take on a life of their own, which accounts for the fact that other people don't perceive them as Jodie preaching.

Nell was a bit of both sorts of films. It's the story of a back-woods wild child who speaks her own forty-word language. The role of Nell was one of the most challenging an actress can attempt. It doesn't allow for hiding behind makeup, props, action scenes, or flashy costumes. As producer of the film, Jodie came to the typically self-confident conclusion that she couldn't trust any actress but herself. Meticulous as ever about details, she picked British *Gorillas in the Mist* director Michael Apted to helm the production, knowing that she already had her work cut out with the acting. And she picked as costars the classically trained *Schindler's List* actor Liam Neeson and his real-life wife, Natasha Richardson.

As producer, director, and CEO of Egg Productions, Jodie may be bossy, but her style of management is far from the old-fashioned, male-oriented, top-down structure. Although she is in charge, she uses a corporate organization that is more circular than linear. The action of making movies revolves around her; she prefers to be in the center of the action rather than above it. When employees come to Jodie's office for a meeting, she immediately comes from behind her desk, pulls a chair out to the middle of the room, and forms a semicircle. In some ways it is symbolic, but her staff knows they are not simply going to get their marching orders, but are going to participate in a planning session where their frank opinions are expected.

On the other hand, there is no mistaking the fact Jodie relishes her new position. "The thing about being in control is: it's a lot more fun than not being in control," she laughs.

Because every aspect of the business is so familiar, Jodie likes to have a hand in every facet of the creative, and even the business, side. Egg is run by unusually specific and rigid rules for a show business operation. The planning and carrying out of film projects is expected to go like clockwork, which is very much in Jodie's character. Even at Yale she was proud to say she never had to do an all-nighter to finish a paper or prepare for an exam. As a student she worked from nine in the morning until six in the evening, then had fun with her friends. It's the same with her productions. There are never any last-minute finishes. Movies are brought in on time and within budget.

Jodie's passion for planning allows her to concentrate on the work of directing once shooting starts. When she is on location, the rule is that only one production person is allowed to contact her directly by phone and then only during business hours. Everyone else has to use e-mail, which has become one of her favorite ways to communicate: it's efficient and impersonal.

Always hidden behind darkly tinted windows when she drives around Los Angeles, and dark sunglasses when she walks, Jodie couldn't be more opposite the character of Nell. Nell is a true innocent, an unsophisticated, unsocialized girl who grew up in the wilderness of North Carolina with her hermit mother. Just a toddler when her mother suffered a stroke that severely affected her speech, Nell had contact with no one else and learned only fractured words. When her mother died, she was discovered by a country doctor, played by Liam Neeson.

Nell is studied by Natasha Richardson, a research psychologist who finds her unsocialized behavior at once startling and fascinating. Jodie saw Nell as "emotionally available," something she has personally striven to avoid her whole life. "She doesn't know that you're supposed to cover things up or be ashamed or change the way you react to something based on what someone might think of you. I thought it was going to be awful. I thought it was really going to be hard, and I was going to be miserable."

Nell reacts, or in normal terms, overreacts, wildly to every stimulus. In one scene she dances in a crowded pool hall and suddenly pulls her dress up to her neck, unashamedly exposing herself. And several times she swims in the nude, her body glistening in the moonlight. Both scenes lack any feeling of prurience, instead showing how unencumbered Nell is of social restrictions. The scenes are very unlike Jodie. But something about playing Nell freed Jodie from her usual inhibitions. Being a good actor had always been the primary way in which Jodie found approval and kept the world in order. The result was a mesmerizing performance. Nell's joy is explosive, her fear staggering. Her heart and soul are reflected clearly in her almost feral eyes. Exulting in the role, Jodie howls, whirls, and dances madly, using her body in new ways to convey panic, rage, incomprehension, and frustration.

An important part of Jodie's portrayal of the role is that Nell couldn't possibly have possessed the facial codes—smiles, frowns, and looks of empathy—we use to express emotions and communicate. Jodie had to unlearn all the normal reactions we use in real life and that actors use on camera to portray feelings. Interestingly, those communication tools had come phenomenally easy to Jodie as a child.

When she first decided to go ahead with the project, she was understandably anxious. "I realized there was no amount of research that was going to tell me how to do it. And I realized that I was either going to fail miserably or I was gonna find it, and no amount of worrying about it was gonna make it happen."

As producer, Jodie decided *Nell* needed her own unique language, so she hired *Shadowlands* writer William Nicholson to help write one, as well as to rewrite the script, which was based on Mark Handley's play *Idioglossia*. As soon as the movie was released, the weird burbling and cooing noises they dreamed up slipped into the language as buzz-words, and several years later some of the sounds, like *chicko-bee*, are still slang in many places.

Part of the attraction of the script was that one of Jodie's French new-wave cinema heroes, François Truffaut, had made a film called *Wild Child* in 1969, retelling the true story of Victor, the wild boy of Aveyron, who was found living in a French forest during the eighteenth century. Truffaut also acted in his version of the tale, playing the well-meaning doctor who tried to "civilize" the boy. The French director and Jodie thought the story should be about the corruption of an innocent by civilization.

An important difference between the two films is that Victor's story ended badly: he was institutionalized once the public lost interest in his case. Nell was granted a happier fate. Though she doesn't learn English, the doctors learn her language, which is accepted as a valid, useful tongue and is not rejected out of hand as gibberish.

The film, representing the greatest risk of Jodie's career, was a great victory. Though she didn't win another Academy Award, director Michael Apted paid Jodie the greatest compliment possible, saying she was able to truly become another person in the role of Nell.

"It was one of those performances that if you don't get it right, it's laughable," said Apted. "And she managed to give a great performance without your ever realizing that it's Jodie Foster. She doesn't implant her fingerprints all over it."

Jodie's fingerprints were all over her next film, though.

Home for the Holidays was a labor of love that took nearly three years to complete. When she was finally preparing to begin filming during the spring of 1995, Jodie sent me several revisions of the script with notes saying she thought I would relate to the wacky, dysfunctional family it portrayed. As I read succeeding drafts of the *Holidays* scripts, I realized that she was struggling to capture the essence of our strengths and weaknesses as a family. However, in interviews promoting the film, Jodie insisted that our family was completely different from the family in *Holidays*, and that the movie wasn't autobiographical. We certainly were different in some of the specifics. We never had a loopy aunt who gives away lamps; there were few Thanksgivings with a father around. But the general tone of the relationships had much in common with our family.

In one interview Jodie said there was never any screaming in our family, which caused me almost to fall out of my chair. The brittle relations, the tightly wound personalities ready to explode—I could relate to everything in *Holidays*. It *was* us. The characters were changed to protect the guilty, but it was a tongue-in-cheek homage to our family, as any one of us could tell by watching.

I had a hard time watching *Holidays* the first time. In fact, I almost walked out of the theater. The only logical reason for her to so vehemently deny the film was about our family was to avoid embarrassing us, holding us up to ridicule. Because in a sense she did just that, though that certainly wasn't her intent.

Jodie's friend Holly Hunter, who plays Claudia Larson, got glowing reviews as the put-upon daughter (who reminded me a bit of Jodie and her role in our family).

Claudia has just been fired from her job and told by her teenage daughter that she plans to lose her virginity over the weekend, as she goes home to Baltimore for Thanksgiving. When she is picked up at the airport by her parents, played by Charles Durning and Anne Bancroft, she passes a man speaking on a pay phone, rolling his eyes in weariness over the impending family drama. A few minutes later, as Claudia sits in the back of her parents' car while they talk at each other, she glances into the car in the next lane. The pay-phone man is now undergoing the same torture with his parents. The actor is Jodie's good friend Randy Stone. He is her stand-in, suffering alongside Claudia.

Anne Bancroft (who one critic said reinvented Mrs. Robinson twenty-eight years later) also bore a passing resemblance to Mom, particularly the way she can get under your skin until you want to scream. She's the kind of tough, loyal mother you'd want beside you if, say, you were facing down the Mongol hordes with a flyswatter. But she's not the person to turn to when you're seeking a little serenity.

As for Charles Durning's Dad, he's there, all right, but in many ways he isn't. Adrift in his retirement, he's disconnected and purposeless enough that he has largely stopped playing a role in the family, except as a source of worry for his wife. The fact that the father of the family can't manage the basic job of carving the turkey, which starts a chain of events that lead to a huge blowup and estrangement within the family, seems to me to be pretty symbolic of a story we Fosters know well.

Jodie has admitted that the three young people in the movie, Claudia, Joanne, and Tommy, are "three different parts of me." I was most struck by the conflict between easygoing, artsy Claudia and her tightly wound, responsibility-fixated sister, Joanne. Joanne feels that she's spent her whole life bearing the burden of her family's inadequacies. Her gay brother Tommy is a public embarrassment, and her sister Claudia got all the attention because she was artistic. Now that their aging parents seem to require more and more attention, Joanne feels the whole burden descending on her. Her life has always been limited by these people, it's not getting any better, and she's so angry about the whole thing that she seems beyond reconciliation.

Claudia is simply struggling to live her own life yet maintain the affection she feels for her sometimes trying parents and siblings. She knows she isn't as close to them as she'd like to be, but she's also aware that staying out of the family pressure cooker isn't such a bad idea. She sees what's happening to Joanne and can't understand why her sister doesn't define herself as more than the sum of her family relationships.

It's Jodie, the gifted child who has always carried more than her weight in the family, versus the Jodie who has gotten on with her life but hasn't left everything behind.

As for Tommy, he has also created a life apart from his family, going so far as to hide some of the most important parts of that life even from Claudia, who adores him. Though he loves to tease Joanne and her husband, he clearly bears deep affection for his parents. So the separateness of his life is more acutely uncomfortable than what Claudia has achieved. I thought of how Jodie's mind has always taken her places none of the rest of us were interested in going—or maybe even able to follow. Mom shared many but not all of her interests, but only Dad comes near her intellect. Since she has sealed him out of her life, she inhabits two worlds in the way that Tommy does, with no bridge between them. Though she is always welcome in the family, she knows that there are many parts of her that none of the rest of us can fully comprehend.

Home for the Holidays also deals with many issues our family has been facing recently. Our parents are aging, and Mom has been in poor health lately, a constant source of worry for all of us. Dad, who has, thankfully, made his peace with Mom and now talks on the phone to her for endless hours, has been particularly concerned about her. He is in his seventies, and she is fast approaching hers, so it is on the one hand great to see they have put the past behind them, but sad they couldn't have done it back when they had four little children. Of course, so much of what we became was shaped by the domestic turmoil we grew up with. If they had been Ozzie and Harriet, Jodie would now be a doctor or a college professor.

Fortunately, we all try to accept each other for what we are and have become. Our sibling rivalry has been going on since we were toddlers, and isn't likely to stop. Our individual quirks still grate sometimes when we get together. After all these years, the reunions still aren't easy, though we are getting better.

The most recent Foster family gathering was at Thanksgiving in Jodie's rented house in Los Angeles. The house is an L-shaped, modernist, white-washed cement block affair with a staircase that winds up the side. The floors are all burnished hardwood, covered with tan throw rugs. Nearly all the furniture came with the house. The only things Jodie brought along were her kitchen gear and some fine Irish linen, one indulgence she got from Mom. Everything else is basically Crate and Barrel, revealing nothing about the current occupant. There's a small lap pool in the back and a fire pit for barbecue, both of which Jodie uses a great deal.

One of the few personal touches is hidden in the small basement, where free weights, Stairmasters, and mirrors bear testament to Jodie's concern with personal fitness. Cedar closets containing her treasure trove of free Giorgio Armani clothes vie for space with the workout equipment.

The area of the house Jodie most cares about is the kitchen. Her Calphalon pots and pans hang from the ceiling or adorn the butcher-block tables, as do all manner of wire whips and whisks, butcher knives, spatulas, basters, mills, shears, graters, sieves, mortars, and pestles.

The kitchen is a place she believes needs to be run as carefully as mission control. Just as she gets rid of gifts and clothes, Jodie unclutters her kitchen, and even friends' kitchens, the same way. She has a curious habit of opening up a pantry and warily eyeing the pull dates on the canned goods, furrowing her brow occasionally, separating them into three groups. The purpose is to throw away cans with expired dates, to return those with a long shelf life remaining to the back of the shelf, and to make a group of cans that should be watched carefully because their time is nigh.

That holiday, watching my sister working in her kitchen with the skill and economy of motion befitting a master chef, reminded me she could have done just about anything she set her mind to. Her cooking is done with the same meticulous attention to detail and inventiveness apparent in her acting and directing. Turkey dinner was incredibly good, a labor of love for Jodie, who has no servants or help in the kitchen.

Cindy and her children, fourteen-year-old Alexandre and nine-year-old Amanda, were in Paris. Connie, her husband, Bob Edmundson, who is a lawyer in the Los Angeles area, and Connie's sons, Chadwick Dunn, ten, and Christian Dunn, eighteen, were skiing. So the family members present were just Mom, my wife Stacy, her mom, Margaret, me, and Jodie. Filling the table were some of Jodie's friends from Egg Films—including Randy Stone. Production on *Home for the Holidays* was supposed to be starting soon, so the Egg folks videotaped and shot endless stills of our gathering to use in planning the movie.

The upcoming movie became a hot topic of conversation. It was only Jodie's second directing job and the first she wasn't acting in as well, which meant she could concentrate all her efforts behind the camera. It was a heady moment for her to be on the verge of heading up a production that was entirely her responsibility.

Mom was more interested in talking about Connie's and Cindy's marital problems. They had both recently divorced, and Mom didn't much care for either Cindy's ex-husband or Connie's present spouse, though she had suddenly fallen madly in love with Connie's ex and insists she's a fool not to go back to him, or at least call him, or something. (I zone out when the screed begins.) Cindy's situation was unique enough to dominate a good part of the dinner conversation. She and her husband had agreed to a divorce, but neither one was willing to move out of their Paris house. Since divorces in France can take years to be finalized, they divided the living areas in the house, just like Michael Douglas and Kathleen Turner in *War of the Roses*. Naturally, Mom was outraged that her husband didn't give in to all of Cindy's demands and move out.

In the midst of Mom's harangue on the fools who thought they were good enough to marry her children, Jodie smiled waggishly at Stacy and said, "Thank God the only one she has ever liked is Stacy." My wife looked toward the heavens and said amen. Stacy *is* the only one of my three wives who has ever been invited nongrudgingly to family gatherings, despite the fact that I had three children with the others. In fact, Mom likes Stacy so much she made it clear to me in advance that if anything happened between us, she would unhesitatingly take her side.

In the past at family gatherings, Jodie has usually been the little queen on the throne, offering learned opinions on every topic that comes up, whether she knows anything about it or not. She has always pontificated, playing the brainy, studious, overly analytical woman/child. Over the years the control-freak act, which she has always been the first to admit she played to a T, was simply a part of her personality that we were all used to.

But in the last few years she appears to have had an epiphany. Now that Jodie *is* the boss on the set, she no longer feels she has to act that way with her friends and family. It was wonderful at Thanksgiving to see the new Jodie. She was laid-back, letting the evening flow with no attempt to dominate or manage the conversation. Instead, after racing around the house, cheerfully serving a five-course feast, she cleaned up and did the dishes, with help from everybody, and finally took off her apron, relaxed on a couch with a glass of champagne, her second and last of the night.

One of the banes of our family get-togethers has always been talk of politics. It's the one topic sure to cause a shouting match and a premature end to the evening. More than once the less politically committed family members have headed for the door quickly, fleeing a nascent screaming match over anything from Eisenhower to the Gulf War to Ross Perot. The arcane political points have often been comprehensible only to Mom. My feeling is that I left home at fifteen to avoid that kind of chaos, so I'm not about to listen to it now.

At the Thanksgiving dinner, we were able to end the evening without a major blowup, which is rather unusual. The previous Easter Sunday, after another dinner at Jodie's, we hadn't been so lucky. We thought we were actually in the clear, and were all getting ready to leave when three friends of Jodie's showed up at the door. They were hip, sexy-looking young women dressed in fashionably punkish clothes, with cropped hair. One had a tattoo, another a nose ring. In other words, they had the look that Mom considers slovenly. Unable to control herself, she hissed at Jodie: "*What are they doing here? You should know better than that!*" Unfortunately, it was said loud enough that the young women could hardly have missed it.

A look of hot anger shot across Jodie's face. She was embarrassed and furious, but knew there was nothing she could do. If her friends had come a few minutes later, we would have been safely gone and the incident wouldn't have occurred. Summoning all her considerable skills as an actress, Jodie politely introduced everyone, though I'm sure she would have preferred to have said Mom was a stranger who had just wandered in. Stiffly, the rest of us mumbled greetings and made for the door.

When Mom gets home after a domestic fiasco like that, she will call Jodie and apologize, but her apologies always seem to end with a rejoinder like "But if you had done as I told you . . ." I don't know if Jodie even bothers to hope anymore that someday Mom won't insist on having the last word. I've certainly given up. And I think we've both learned, as Claudia does in *Home for the Holidays*, that conflicts in families are often never really won and that the sanest course is sometimes not to try.

One important and revealing way in which I think *Home for the Holidays* differed from Jodie's personal outlook also bears mention. Joanne's odious little daughter is an object of torture for Tommy and incomprehensible to Claudia. Jodie, on the other hand, is very close to her young nephews, Connie's boys Christian and Chadwick. She has been like a second mother to them over the years, picking them up at school, taking them out, and enjoying watching them grow up. They are a very important part of her life.

Since they were very little, Jodie has created little improvised playlets for them. She plays all the roles, sometimes four or five, switching voices and expressions, putting on different hats and scarves, and just driving them crazy. She's so good at it, grown-ups get caught up as well. But it's basically a game she devised for their pleasure. Though they're older now, they still enjoy it.

Jodie has grown up a lot since her bitter words all those years ago in Georgia about the failure of our family. That's the danger in writing about anyone as young as Jodie. The weight of her experiences, while important, can seem to overwhelm the evolving ways she adapts to them. Whether making *Home for the Holidays* will provide her the kind of catharsis on family relationships that *The Accused* and *Silence of the Lambs* gave her on victimization, I can't say. But she's taken a step in the right direction.

Home for the Holidays was, like *Nell*, a labor of love. It would have been nice if the films had made a lot of money, but that wasn't the goal Jodie had in mind. She wanted to succeed artistically and to tell the truth about something important to her.

Holidays was a low-budget film, and it wound up paying for itself, even showed a reasonable profit after overseas sales, videocassette, and cable sales were counted. And the reviews were at least mixed. Jodie was praised for "masterful direction" by syndicated writer John Larsen, who also called the cast "all splendid." But in the end Larsen and most of the critics found *Holidays* lacking. "It's not a great movie, and in some respects it's not even a good movie. But it's an okay movie as long as you don't set your sights too high."

It was an ironic jab, because Jodie always sets her sights impossibly high, and when she stumbles it is always a painful fall.

FIFTEEN

*I'm tired of people always trying to psycho-
analyze me.* —JODIE FOSTER

W hereas most stars are subjected to interviews asking
nosy questions about their love life, writers inter-
viewing Jodie tend to go far afield, trying to plumb the
depths of her psyche. Part of the reason for the intrusiveness
is that unlike most stars, who are unveiled to the public as
fully formed creatures, Jodie was presented as an embryonic
creation.

She came on the world stage as a toddler peddling
Coppertone suntan lotion. And the majority of people
believe that Jodie appeared bare-bottomed in the ads. The
truth is that only in the billboard painting of a child, who
resembled Jodie, was the bathing suit pulled down by a
frisky puppy, revealing a tan line. Both the Coppertone
people and Jodie have expressed annoyance over the years at

the persistent myth, but it is a falsehood that refuses to go away.

The person as public image became in succession a precocious preschooler, a rambunctious grade-school child, a saucy nymphet, a world-weary Ivy Leaguer, and finally a woman of distinct purpose and presence. Because this transformation has been so visible, people feel they know Jodie personally and are as entitled to her secrets as her best friend.

The Hollywood movie industry has watched her grow up as well. She is one of the best known, if little understood, actors in the business. Over the course of almost fifty films and countless hours of TV, Jodie has seen everybody come and go, the parking spaces and office spaces change, the in restaurants come and go. At thirty-four she is already a major survivor. The only comparable contemporary star is Elizabeth Taylor. But Liz has played out her private life in public as though it were an eighteenth-century French bedroom farce. Her marriages and divorces, couplings and uncouplings, gurney rides in and out of hospitals, wobbling in and tottering out of rehabilitation clinics, and sundry other public dramas have been carried on in our living rooms, thanks to tabloids and TV. Because Jodie hasn't carried on for them in like fashion, the press demands to know why. Her incredulous, dismayed response has always been: I don't really do anything.

It's a source of frustration to her fans that Jodie refuses to bare her soul on TV talk shows, and to Hollywood party givers that she refuses to make the circuit even occasionally. Jodie already feels she is too exposed as it is. Her wish would be to make movies yet remain anonymous. When the occasional mad bleatings from Hinckley manage to escape his cell and the press gives them ink, copycat crazies come crawling out to send Jodie obscene threats. When that happens, she has no choice but to retreat from public life completely for a while, curtail her normal life, and hire expensive security guards, in case that one in a million wacko actually tries to carry out his mad fantasy.

To some Jodie's caution may seem to verge on paranoia, but the weirdness she inspires in fans is real and ongoing. In late 1995 she was the subject of some bizarre "internet trash talk," according to her lawyer, Matthew Saver. Apparently, it wasn't a threat against her life but filthy, "aggressive sexual talk" about her, including mention of rape and defecation. Copies of the material were turned over to the FBI, and Jodie was assured there was no danger. Still, simply knowing some anonymous sicko out there is having thoughts like that about her and sharing them in a public forum is upsetting. He could be in Alaska or in West Hollywood. It could be "twelve-year-old prepubescent babble" as Saver characterized it, or the yearnings of a psychopath.

These days Jodie still lives a carefully balanced and controlled life, largely in Los Angeles, with occasional trips for work and pleasure. When she travels on her own impulse, she most often goes to New York. The differences between the cities please her for different reasons. Los Angeles is where she was raised, and she's steeped in many aspects of its culture; her heart is there. New York appeals to her head, to her professional and intellectual ambitions. Despite the call from many people she respects to abandon L.A. for New York, I don't think she will. It's one of the few times when her heart will win out over her head.

The films Jodie wants to make, though, are far more New York in style than L.A. Martin Scorsese, Woody Allen, Robert DeNiro, and others like them are more kindred to Jodie than, say, Sylvester Stallone or Arnold Schwarzenegger. Given her exasperation with the big studios, Jodie would have no qualms about leaving them behind to make the leap to New York, where serious people make serious movies.

And Jodie loves much of what the city has to offer. She enjoys wandering in and out of galleries and workshops in SoHo and Williamsburg, maintaining her acquaintance with the world of artists Andy Warhol introduced her to after she struck up a friendship with him following her *Interview* appearance. In New York, too, she can indulge her love of foreign films in a way she can no place else. Over the years she has developed an encyclopedic knowledge of movies from India, Russia, China, and most of the rest of the world.

Yet as much as Jodie delights in wandering about Manhattan and riding the subways, inevitably some of the supposedly jaded New Yorkers begin to stare. Jodie has always, when confronted by a stranger who asks if she is *the* Jodie Foster, vehemently denied it. She doesn't necessarily think anybody believes the fib, but it seems to confuse them long enough for her to get away.

Clara Lisa Kabbaz, who has known Jodie since they were students at the Lycée Français, says, "I think Jodie would give anything to remain inconspicuous for the rest of her life." And that's the real reason why New York will never really snare Jodie: it throws you into contact with people at every junction.

"The idea that on the New York streets thirty to thirty-five people would look at me every day and there's nothing I could do about it drives me nuts! Everybody looks at your body. Come on! It's embarrassing," Jodie says, speaking like a true Angeleno, accustomed to the isolation of cars.

New York does offer the one realm of acting where Jodie has yet to make a mark: the stage. Yet there is always the lingering memory of her time on the boards of Yale. Somewhere out there in the dark audience, which Jodie couldn't see because of the footlights, lurked Hinckley's doppelgänger, hoping to finish the looney's work by killing Jodie. Movies, after all, are made behind high fences, with armed guards and assistants carrying walkie-talkies to make sure everything is running smoothly and most of all to make sure strangers aren't on the set. Theaters, by their nature, are packed with strangers.

But just as important are Jodie's aesthetics of performance. She is far too steeped in the culture of movies to be comfortable in front of a live audience. She doesn't like the fact that the audience can be looking at any part of the actors or the scene they want. She thinks granting that much freedom is going too far. With movies the director decides how much of a scene or an actor the viewer can see. In fact, that limitation is part of the dramatic power of films. What is in the darkened basement, or around the corner, that you can't see is often more powerful than what you can see. Theater doesn't contain that visual dynamic and, simply put, Jodie would feel far too naked to the audience on a stage.

There are others reasons why Jodie will continue to favor the West Coast. She thinks New York is too intense to put up with all the time. In an uncharacteristic flash of self-doubt she says, "I don't dress well enough. I'm not good-looking enough. I'm not in enough. Even when you get hip enough, then they change it, and you've got to be even hipper. I can't keep up with it." Then, too, though Mom is no longer involved professionally in Jodie's career, the bond of a lifetime is still there; it would kill her if her baby daughter moved to the East Coast.

Of course, Hollywood has its own chic trappings and attitudes, and Jodie defies those as well. Her usual outfit is a man's white T-shirt, dark skirt, sandals, no makeup, and tousled hair. The only clothes she buys are the casual, comfortable kind. She has never bought designer clothes in her life and never will. The Armani dresses and suits she wears to the Oscars and premiere parties are given to her.

For years she eschewed the emblem of Hollywood citizenship, a cellular phone. Driving around town on her personal errands was for her a time to think, work out plots and dialogue, or just to blast the radio. Quintessential L.A. girl that she is, Jodie loves to ply the freeways and spend time isolated and totally unavailable. In fact, she often has lunch or even dinner in her car, hiding behind dry cleaning hanging over the windows. No one can come up and ask for an autograph or spoil her meal by staring.

But her business partners went ballistic over the lack of a car phone. They acted as though the sky might fall if an hour went by that she couldn't be reached. Reluctantly she has started carrying one, but the power switch mostly remains off. Don't call me, and it's doubtful I'll call you, is her motto.

One piece of modern technology Jodie has taken to is the personal computer. She uses a Macintosh LC III in her office and is something of a wizard with it. On the road she always has some version of a laptop at hand for e-mail, fax, or to download information from data banks.

On a film set Jodie gets up at dawn or before, but at home she likes to sit up most nights and watch movies, mostly foreign, on her VCR. Close friends and relatives all know that it is verboten to call before ten in the morning. I think if Egg Pictures was on fire in the morning, they would wait until after ten to call her. Staying up late and sleeping are her "one indulgence" in a life where she allows herself few.

Jodie also lingers in Southern California because she likes the weather, the beaches, the hills and canyons where we grew up. Every day when there is time, she runs three and a half miles around a track in the hills. Vowing never to get fat again—even though she knows she no longer has to put up with cigar-chomping producers wanting to see her body to make sure she is thin enough for their movies—she works out constantly. Weights, Stairmasters, and treadmills must be available whether she is in one of her rented homes, on location, or staying in hotels during publicity tours.

In the past four years or so, fitness has become a compulsion. Jodie says she works out not so much to build muscles or lose weight as to recover from the stress of acting, directing, and producing. "To act is to experience powerlessness. It really kills my confidence. I get torn down from it, and I need to build up again. I start working out again like crazy after making a movie. It's not about exercise, it's regenerating a sense of self."

That evanescent sense of self may seem very unlike the Jodie who has survived so much, but in a 1991 interview with *Rolling Stone* magazine, Jodie told the writer she had been "obsessing" about William Styron's book *Darkness Visible*, the story of his long struggle with severe clinical depression. She marveled that depression can come suddenly "in the midst of everything." The abyss of severe depression "is a place that awaits everyone, and you either end up there or not." And she confided her own frightening brush with depression: "I've been *there*. Styron was put away, I was not."

Striving, Jodie says, is about working out ways to keep from falling into the gaping maw of hopelessness and gloom; that is one of the keys to understanding human behavior. Certainly her experience with Hinckley brought home to her the transitory aspects of existence. Anybody she passes on the street who gives that quizzical look of recognition could be a crazy ready to end her life. Yet one of Jodie's strengths is her ability to see the big picture and understand what she must accept in life and what she can reasonably hope to control or change.

Her pervasive need for privacy sometimes works in strange ways. For instance, despite the fact that she considers herself a feminist and most of her friends go to female gynecologists, she goes to a male one. The reason, she says only half tongue in cheek, is that a woman doctor would see through any subterfuge, any attempt to hide her secret fears. Jodie doesn't want a relationship that intimate with anyone.

She feels the same way about female directors, whom she has avoided. She did do *Siesta*, which was directed by Mary Lambert, but their relationship has been a bit rocky. While Jodie was directing *Little Man Tate*, producer Scott Rudin watched the dailies and said he thought a close-up should be added to the scene. More than slightly piqued at the suggestion, Jodie quipped, "Why don't you get Mary Lambert to come in?"

A friend of Lambert's on the set repeated the crack, causing the director to whip off a caustic note to which Jodie had to make an apologetic reply.

When Jodie was making *Carny* in 1980, a friend asked if she would prefer to work with a woman director. "Not if I can help it," she replied. "That's because women can see right through you. They're smarter than men; you can't con them. When the director is a man you can say"—she switches to a little-girl voice—" 'Oh, gee, is it okay if I take an extra ten minutes for lunch?' But not with a woman. They never let you get away with that."

Much has changed since that 1991 interview when Jodie talked about the imminence of depression. She is now head of her own company. Being successful and earning good money isn't what matters, though, but that she is in charge. Jodie's darkest moments have always been tied to the threat that other people were stifling or squashing her independence. She now has the financial and psychological resources to resist those threats.

Her forthcoming movie, *Contact*, based on a Carl Sagan novel about a brilliant young scientist who learns how to communicate with extraterrestrials through radio telescope, has spiritual quest as an important subtext. "It deals with faith, how wonder propels us all. How wonder is the basis of all spiritual experience," Jodie says.

Contact became mired in problems when Jodie, who as star has script approval, flatly rejected a draft written by Menno Meyjes (*The Color Purple*) and approved by director George Miller (*Mad Max*). The producing studio, Warner

Brothers, immediately suggested that Jodie drop out of the project. Rather than be cowed by the threat, Jodie came up with a new version of the script, which she insisted on reading to Miller. The director hated it and dropped out himself. Resolute in her desire to make the film, she went back to the studio and fought for her script, and a new director who would follow it. After a fight she prevailed and gained a say in choosing the new director, and signed Hollywood's hottest new face, Matthew McConaughey, as her costar.

I studied astronomy when I took courses at El Camino College in Los Angeles, which though a small college had a very good observatory. I fell in love with gazing in wonder at the universe. Jodie has also been fascinated by the subject for years, so she and I talked about astronomy a great deal at the time. When she became involved with the Sagan book a few years ago, she called with excitement in her voice to say she had found the perfect story about the topic. As always, she plunged into it for all she was worth, planning to become an expert on the subject.

In the four years Egg Pictures has been up and running, the volume of their output has been somewhat less than what had been hoped for, partly because Jodie is naturally cautious and meticulous. But this is also due to a paucity of good scripts, particularly in terms of strong women's roles. Jodie says she has read everything that's out there, and "it's a bad year for women." For years, trying her hand at short stories and doing major rewriting jobs on scripts has been an avocation, so it seems only a matter of time before she solves the problem herself. I know what would make her proudest is to be a film auteur like her French new-wave cinema idols

François Truffaut, Claude Chabrol, and Louis Malle, who wrote their screenplays and directed them.

Yet whether she adds screenwriter to the titles of director, producer, star, or not, Jodie is going to stay in the business for the rest of her life, because she is passionately, completely committed to the film business now. "Even if I tried to be divorced from films, I couldn't 'cause that's what I grew up doing. It would be like cutting off my right arm. I don't know what I would be if I didn't have that outlet. Acting is the perfect craft for the two-personality person," she laughs.

What does worry her is that the worst time for a woman actor is after the age of forty, because Hollywood is still so appearance-conscious. Even with her talents, she's aware that when it comes to acting, everyone is judged on looks. Mom has always insisted there will be plenty of mature roles once Jodie is past thirty-five. But Jodie is cautious about relying on the kindness of Hollywood.

"There is the awkward transition when all the sages decide that you're too old to be the love interest," she says. "I don't want to feel bad about myself when I turn forty. If I can't play the part, then I will direct."

In another scenario that Jodie floats from time to time, France is a very strong magnet. For a long time she has threatened to move there toward the end of her thirties. Of late she has been spending more and more time in France and has grown close again to our sister Cindy, who lives there with her family. In the next six or seven years that might happen. But I don't take Jodie's speculations on her future too seriously, because they change almost daily.

Her best friend John Hutman acknowledges, "Jodie is a

planner. She has a one-week plan, a one-year plan, and a five-year plan, and none of them comes true, but she believes in them wholeheartedly at the time."

Jodie knows that burnout is a real possibility if she continues pushing herself to the limit. "I know I will slow down," she admits. "There is only so long you can do this without becoming a strange person." She has spent a lifetime trying not to be strange, to be a normal person despite everything. "You want people to think you are like them. You have to fight to be open-minded, to be connected to the world."

Pumping gas, grocery shopping, doing her own laundry, and house cleaning are ways Jodie tries to be connected to reality. "I like chores," she says. "I like picking up the laundry. I don't want to give that up and let someone else do it. That's not living. But it's not easy. I have a lot to do. And there are always friends calling me up to do things. Something's going to have to go. I guess it's going to have to be my friends," she laughs.

Despite her drive and her intellect, life is not all business deals and Kurosawa films. Jodie, of all people, has become a big fan of MTV's *Beavis and Butthead* cartoons. She even does a convincing Beavis cackle. Then again, Jodie always enjoyed Saturday morning cartoons, sitting in her pajamas and watching *Mighty Mouse*. It was strange when we were kids to watch her eat up this segment of pop culture, then retire to her room to read French poetry.

Certainly the time Jodie spent reading has left a more profound mark than whatever she absorbed from Foghorn Leghorn or Johnny Quest. Since her days at the lycée, Jodie's favorite poet has been Charles-Pierre Baudelaire. He described himself as a "seeker of God without religious beliefs," searching in the color of a flower, or the frown of a prostitute, for the true meaning of life. Jodie has said many times that failure is a much better teacher than success: the short, miserable life of Baudelaire was a case study in failure. Her favorite among his works is his masterpiece *Les fleurs du mal* (*Flowers of Evil*), which was deemed obscene and blasphemous in nineteenth-century France. Melancholy and dark, the poems were influenced by Edgar Allan Poe, whose work Baudelaire translated and emulated. Now considered among the best of French poetry, the work was banned and never published in full until 1949, nearly a hundred years after Baudelaire died bankrupt, disdained, and shunned.

Another significant influence has been Toni Morrison, who was the subject of Jodie's senior thesis at Yale. (Though Morrison would become the first African-American woman to win the Nobel Prize for literature, Jodie's interest in her predated that recognition, as well as the Pulitzer Prize she won for *Beloved*.) Morrison's works combine African folk tales, African and Western mythology, plus the influence of William Faulkner and other Southern writers, to compassionately explore the lives of black women. In *The Bluest Eye* (1970) she tells the story of a little black girl who yearns to see the world through the eyes of a little white girl. *Beloved* is a haunting tale of slavery and its consequences, particularly with regard to family relationships, set in rural Ohio, where Morrison herself was born and raised.

One of the advantages of fame, of course, is that other accomplished people will take your phone call. Jodie had admired Toni Morrison for years, and when she decided to make the writer's work the subject of her thesis, she sought to contact her. Morrison immediately responded and talked to her at great length about her work, which for Jodie was a dream come true. When it was submitted, Jodie's thesis was given the highest praise by Yale's literature faculty, and Jodie was encouraged to have it published. Unfortunately, Morrison refused to give permission to publish the work, a source of puzzlement and disappointment to Jodie, though, naturally, she complied with Morrison's wishes.

Morrison's work is summed up by writer Walter Mosley: "Toni is always writing about what's going on underneath the kind of experience of sexism or racism or class issues . . . that agony, the elation beneath those experiences. She kind of peels back the world and lets you look inside it even if you thought you knew it before."

Like Baudelaire, Morrison speaks to Jodie's primal instincts about society and womankind's place in it. In her book *Song of Solomon*, Morrison writes:

> The pride, the conceit of these doormat women amazed him. They were always women who had been spoiled children. Whose whims had been taken seriously by adults and who grew up to be the stingiest, greediest people on earth and out of their stinginess grew their stingy little love that ate everything in sight.

Jodie's post-Yale film work has been greatly influenced by Morrison's insights and probably will be even more so now that she has control over her movies. Obviously, she would love to bring one or more of Morrison's novels to the screen. Morrison is extremely particular about allowing her very personal and "richly complex, sensuously conveyed images of events, characters, and moods" (the words used by the Nobel committee) to be adapted for a commercial movie, even by an admirer. But Jodie was allowed to get close to the author and to show Morrison that she has a grasp of the spirit of her work. That gives her hope of getting a screenplay written based on one of the six novels, and maybe even a cast chosen that might reach Morrison's high standards. That's the kind of mountain Jodie would like to scale.

SIXTEEN

Most of my movies are about the making of heroines.   —JODIE FOSTER

Jodie has always had a deep sense of responsibility toward her family. She has gotten used to that burden, and is happy that now she can afford to take care of Mom as she gets older. She knows she could pay for a major operation if someone in the family needed it. It sounds almost trivial that a wealthy star should measure things in such a way, but the fortune Jodie has made and continues to make is there precisely for that kind of security, to make sure she never again has to live through the dark, frightful nights of our childhood. She will be the master of her fate, not the victim of it.

As for the rest of the cast members in the Foster Family Drama Hour, we're all surviving and relatively sane, given what we've been through.

*   *   *

Visiting Los Angeles these days serves to remind me why I moved to Minnesota. The town that I was born in smelled of orange blossoms on a spring day, not noxious fumes that leave you gasping for breath. Stacy and I live on five acres in the woods outside Duluth, in a community where everyone knows their neighbors and their neighbors' children, where it gives me giddy, cackling pleasure to ski through crystalline, virgin snow and to paddle a canoe through the ice-cold water of burbling streams, catch a hefty trout, and set it free.

Stacy and I are planning to have children and raise them in this splendid wilderness. I hope they can find here the rapture I once felt, when California seemed young: running through the orange groves, riding the big red trolley cars with bells trilling as we whizzed over Bunker Hill, the joy that was mine watching my baby sister laugh, pedaling a wobbly paddle boat in Echo Park Lake, while the indulgent sun tanned our bare skin.

Considering all the strange twists and turns my life has taken in the relatively brief time I have been alive, I have to pinch myself when I reflect on how lucky I am to have found such a happy new beginning to my story. For the first time I have found true, unconditional love and a marriage I know will last forever. My business, constructing houses in Minnesota, is satisfying and successful. The winters up here are frigid and unforgiving of the careless, but even working in the snow with beads of ice forming in my hair, which I keep long in the winter to keep my ears warm, it's nice to be far away from the storms I endured in sunny California.

Mom knew when she rolled into Los Angeles, just an awestruck, Rockford, Illinois, teenager, that the city was either going to be her bane or a paradise. She had burned her bridges and couldn't turn back. In that regard she was in the same position as millions of other pilgrims. But unlike most, she had the fire in her belly. She was going to get a house in the hills with Memphis furniture and Herman Miller chairs. She would decorate her walls with the silkscreens of a young man named Andrew Warhola, who at the time was designing Christmas cards in New York. She achieved all that she dreamed of and more: fame, recognition, wealth, and even a degree of clout in Hollywood. It would have been hard to imagine all that when she and a friend from Rockford named Gloria took in the city through tired, road-dust-red eyes.

Over the years Mom and I clashed as strong-willed people do. Perhaps I should have bent more to her desires, stuck with show business, rather than fight it. . . .

Today, I would say our mother is a satisfied person. Like Jodie, she has a very small circle of intimate friends, who have proved their loyalty over a period of many years. She is well aware of her errors and mistakes in judgment over the years. Perhaps she is contrite over some of them, but not, I think, to any great extent. She has not been a person blessed with the luxury of time for self-analysis. Her battles have been to survive, to keep her children fed, clothed, and sheltered. She did whatever it took to accomplish those ends.

In many ways Mom is the archetype of Jodie's persecuted female hero. It's her passion, flaws, and courage that Jodie celebrates in her films. There are many things that she did perfectly. She taught us right from wrong, compassion for victims of discrimination, manners, and the way to muster strength to get up and continue to fight when it seems all is lost. So many kids grow up with much less.

Dad, of course, would never be invited to Jodie's house under any circumstances. I think that's lamentable, but he accepts being frozen out with graceful regret. Connie and Cindy speak to him on rare occasions, but at least they acknowledge him as their father. The irony is that Mom worked so hard on us over the years to hate him, and now she talks to him all the time.

He now lives in the San Fernando Valley, in a far more modest style than his mother's Beverly Hills mansion. At age seventy-five, he still works very hard to support his wife and two children, running his construction business. But judging from the adoring relationship between Dad and his daughters, he has clearly learned a great deal about being a father. It's wonderful that there can be second chances, and redemption. At an age when most people are rocking on the porch, he is scrambling to raise his fourth family, though I don't think he would have it any other way. Foster men and women have a history of living well into their nineties, so he could easily live to see another set of grandchildren.

Through his chats with Mom, he keeps up with what the four of us and his grandchildren are up to, and he wants to know every detail of Jodie's projects. Despite her rejection of him, he is hugely proud of her achievements. He would never say it, but I can't help but think he holds out a distant hope Jodie will come to him, if just for a private talk, before it's too late.

There seems to be nothing hateful or angry in Dad, for all the turmoil and pain in his long life. He holds no grudges and sees everyone's point of view. I see in a new way how opposite he and Mom are in personality and how that conflict is reflected in their children. It's almost a classical struggle between hearts and minds; we have Mom's passionate, take-no-prisoners attitude, as well as Dad's analytical ability to thrust and parry. The individual talents have served us all well—when we have managed not to turn them against each other.

Aunt Jo Dominguez Hill has now been gone for over fifteen years. I wonder if Mom would have finally reconciled with her and if she would have been able to enliven our dutiful holiday gatherings with her wit and humor. Her spirit still burns brightly in all of us, and my sisters and I, and Mom as well, are better people for having known her. I see her gentleness of spirit and compassion in Jodie's art, and in all of our lives.

The fact that she destroyed the tapes of her memoirs indicates to me that she forgave completely at the end the gulf we let open up between us. I will always rue the fact I didn't know about her agonies at the end of her life, and the pain her son Chris and the rest of her wonderful family went through. But that's in the past. Chris and I plan, one day soon, to visit Mt. Lemon, outside Tucson, where he scattered her ashes, to pay tribute to her memory. It's hard to imagine we would have succeeded to the extent we did had it not been for Aunt Jo. I think our family owes everything we have to her generosity, guidance, and love. She was there for us when we desperately needed help and she gave all she had.

*　　*　　*

Understandably, Chris Hill is still bitter over the way his mother was suddenly pushed out of the family, and he has no doubt that the real reason was because her house and her meager income were no longer needed. The depth of his grief over her long, slow death from cancer is written all over his face when he recounts it; it's a palpable thing that will live in him forever. But like Aunt Jo there is no bitterness, only sorrow. Chris has gone through his own torments over the years and suffered emotionally, as we all did, from the domestic convulsions of our early days, but he, too, is a survivor. He lives in Los Angeles, is a skilled carpenter, and is still very close to Jo's family.

My sister Connie lives in Long Beach, California, with her husband, Bob Edmundson, who is a lawyer and an avid surfer, and her two boys by her previous marriage. Their wedding reception was a surf party at a country club, with disc jockeys playing Beach Boys songs. It was the most fun I've had at a wedding. Connie graduated from University of California at Los Angeles and has a very successful interior decorating and design business, with a large clientele. She is the sweetest and kindest person I know; she has always been there for me, with generous help in whatever way it was needed. Connie had a brief acting career, but she wasn't cut out for that sometimes brutal business. She was far too shy and loving.

Our oldest sister, Cindy, went through huge agonies, on a scale with mine. She was the wild child of the family and she paid a steep price for her antics. From the time she was very young she had a rage in her soul. The frequent tempests that washed over our home life seemed to affect Cindy more than the rest of us. She reacted by hurting herself with bursts of anger, lashing out at her siblings, and deliberately doing things to infuriate Mom, who she knew would retaliate with screaming and physical punishment. When she was disciplined she would run away and the cycle would repeat itself. I remember thinking at one of her low points that she would be the first among us to die.

Moving to France changed her life and gave her focus. She's a good teacher and has found her calling. She recently gave birth to a baby girl, who hopefully will center her life further.

And as for Jodie, she continues to astonish. With only a third of her natural life over, she has accomplished an awesome amount. I think her creativity will continue to surprise. And I expect she will branch off into other fields and have a whole new career, in addition to continuing as a filmmaker. Her interests are too vast, and her energy too high, to be bound to any one calling for a lifetime.

Whether she can get over her distrust of intimacy and revulsion over John Hinckley, Jr.'s warped misappropriation of the word *love* is another matter. Mom has spent a lifetime keeping people at a distance and she succeeded all too well. She is now very much alone with her videos and architecture magazines. Jodie seems to be inexorably heading in the same direction sometimes, though I think she is too bright and sees the big picture too well not to realize the traps that await such a choice.

It seems she is just now finding herself as a person. At age thirty-four, she has worked steadily for over thirty years;

many people are thinking about retirement when they have put in that much time. At the peak of her life, Jodie is just now learning how to be playful, silly, and foolish; things she has never been allowed to take the time to do. She says there are many things everybody but her seems to know how to do; being silly is one of them.

Making her first real comedy as an adult, *Maverick*, allowed her to just have nutty fun on a movie for the first time. And developing a friendship with the always wacky Mel Gibson has given her a mentor in monkeyshines. Hopefully now she will allow herself the luxury of watching *Beavis and Butthead* and taking time out for the childhood she was cheated out of because she was helping me support our family from the age of three.

But most of all I think everybody in the family would be ecstatic to hear Jodie announce she had fallen head over heels in love. That would signal for the first time that her heart had won the battle with her head, a fight that has been going on all her life.

Still, reflecting on the first thirty-four years of her life, Jodie says she has very few regrets and a great deal to be grateful for. "I am the luckiest woman alive. But I was not raised normally, I did not grow up in a quote-unquote normal environment. I came up with ways to cope that were right for me, but that have created a character who is immature in a lot of areas, overly wise in others, and stupid about stuff that everybody else can seem to do. There's a whole way of being that I've never experienced because of being a public person."

As a young woman, Jodie was the one member of the family who wasn't fazed by the constant bickering and even the full-tilt scream fests. But now it seems to get to her; in recent years, she doesn't seem to be able to shrug it off nearly as well. She's more prone to pick sides and argue on behalf of issues or people she thinks need defending. She can't stay above the fray as she once did. The stress of her work, now that she has the responsibility of running a multi-million-dollar business as well as being an actress, is getting to her. When the strain of dealing with the family is added, it's just too much.

Yet, much as we all love her, I don't anticipate that any of us are going to suddenly drop behaviors we've developed over the course of our lives. Our passions, our tempers, and our foibles all come with the territory, and the familial attitude is love us or leave us. We've all had our share of stress, and we don't cut each other much slack. Jodie knows that, probably better than any of us. You have to be tough to survive life as a Foster child.

ACKNOWLEDGMENTS

A story was told to me once by the psychologist and writer John Bradshaw that went something like this. A young man had committed suicide, and his soul passed through a tunnel of white light to a room with a large wooden table and chairs. People occupied every chair except one. He sat down in the empty chair and noticed there were big wooden bowls filled with soup. Everybody at the table had big wooden spoons attached to their arms. As the young man looked down, he noticed he had one, too. At first he thought he had been sent to hell, because there was no way he could get the big spoon to his mouth; it was too long. Then a woman directly across the table from him said, without moving her lips, "No, dear, you are in heaven. You see, our spoons are long enough to feed our neighbors." Just at that moment he was medically revived and had a second chance at life.

Writing this book—reliving the experiences of the Foster family—was a tough endeavor emotionally, physically, and spiritually. If not for the support of my family, friends, and God as I understand Her, this book would not have been possible. Therefore, I would like to thank those people with the big wooden spoons.

First, I want to thank Leon Wagener, my cowriter. This book would not have been possible without his skill as a writer and researcher. He lived twenty-four hours a day in my spirit and soul as we wrote, and I will always be grateful for the major contribution he has made to my life. Also, I want to thank his wife, Rochelle Law Wagener, who performed many tasks, including research, contracts, releases, photography, constructive direction, arranging our schedules, and the overall supervising of the project; and Madison Wagener for her great patience and love. Also my literary agent, Denise Marcil, who believed in me, fought for me, and protected me the way a bear protects her cub. The best way to describe my feelings for Denise is to say, If one of those damn New York City cab drivers were about to mow you down in an intersection, I would push you to safety and take the hit myself.

To the whole crew at Dutton Signet, I am grateful to you all and especially my editor, Audrey LaFehr, who believed in my vision from the beginning. Peter Mayer for having faith in me; Elaine Koster and Arnold Dolin for their constructive direction and input; Ed Hernstadt, Alan Kaufman, and the entire legal department, who had their work cut out for them from the beginning; Diane Parke and Lisa Johnson for their compassionate commitment to this project; Leah Bassoff for being that warm voice of communication; and Candace Kodani.

And especially to my soul mate, best friend, lover, and wife, Stacy, for her constructive direction and English skills and whose unconditional love and support for me always warmed my body and soul.

I would also like to thank my children, Lucius V, Brice, and Courtney. I may not have always been the best father, but I am still trying and I will never give up. I love you all so much, and I am very proud of each of you. This book is especially for you.

My family members would have preferred that I not write this book. But I felt a need to tell our story, and I truly believe the truth is a powerful elixir. Mom, Cindy, Connie, and Jodie: I love you all so much and am very proud of each of you. I hope you read this book and understand that none of us would have been the same without our past. If I had a choice to change anything about our family, I would not alter a thing. We are the product of our collective experience, and that has turned out to be pretty good.

Several close friends of Leon's and mine read parts of the manuscript during the process of writing or listened to our thoughts and gave very good and welcome constructive criticism. I give special thanks to Matt Sartwell. The book would not have been the same without his professional contribution.

I'd also like to thank Bryan Sullivan, Susan Maddocks, and the brilliant Gabriel Kelly, who came up with the title *Foster Child* two minutes after the project was described to her.

A big thanks to the people and places that contributed to the book with stories, collaboration, and research: my dear brother, Chris Hill, our father, Lucius F. Foster III, Diana Foster, Toni Kelman, the legendary agent who nourished and guided Jodie's career and mine, Sandy Kelman-Mirisch, Georgina Bowerline, Mrs. Evelyn Almond, the Reverend Marvin Fitz, Nancy Bisbee, the Los Angeles County Court Archives, the Academy of Motion Picture Arts and Sciences Library, Pete Picton, Stewart White, the Rockford, Illinois Public Library History Room, the Screen Actors Guild, the *Los Angeles Times*, the *Sun*, Steve Tinney, and Shirley Chamberlain.

Last but not least, I would like to thank the many people whose names are mentioned in the book and the following people who have also made important contributions to my life and the book; I am eternally grateful to you all. I am sure I have forgotten to mention some people, but they, too, are included in my heart. My legal adviser Irwin Tenenbaum, Jeff Rutherford, Willie Oswald, Melody Bloom, Alex Simms, Dr. Dave Lewis, Paramahansa Yogananda, Randy Braverman, Mark Malloy, Bob Timmons, Carolyn Williams, Polly and Paul Tobias, Eileen Getty, Mark and Mike Redkin, Mark Heffernan, Elliot Prather, Bill Reiby, Tom Ledin, Tom Mellin, Nancy Benninghoff, Don Kienholz, Lynn Bruen, Rhett and Gary Nicholson, Gary Nelson, Pat Longtin, Harvey Solon, William Solon, Margaret Oie, Bill W., Dr. Bob and friends, the crews (you know who you are), PDAP, Le Conte, Bay Street, 27/POP, Samohi, PCNA, Norman's, my friends who have passed away from the ravages of our times, and all of the wonderful friends and people of Duluth, Minnesota.

INDEX